TRIBE OF CANNIBALS

Operation Take-Down America - NY Gulag 10044

by

Deirdre McNamara, D.Hom

With gratitude to all who put their lives on the line to make and keep America free.

That includes those who pray in the silence of their hearts, in lonely solitude as well as those who protect the streets of city and countryside or who sail the swelling seas in battleships or coastguard cutters, and who fly higher than the eagle to watch over and protect the world in company with the foot soldier, on watch at night in hostile territories and terrains, encountering bugs and scorpions and snakes along with IEDs, snipers and tanks, only to be betrayed by the traitors who devour and murder their own, the tribes of cannibals in America and the world, murdering their own children and selling them for profit.

Our decent Americans would weep tears of blood if they truly understood the evils being perpetrated in their name, not only abroad, but right here, on their own home ground.

The globalists, the Davos "private jet set," the Christophobes, alienists, Communists, etc.,.

And then...being Americans, in company with the honest, but more timid nations, they would fight and stop them.

Dedicated to Donald J Trump, 45th President of the USA, First Lady Melania Trump, and family,

and

all Patriots and Pro-Lifers who supported and assisted him in taking on "Operation Take Down America" and winning

OPERATION TAKE BACK AMERICA!

www.deirdresbooks.weebly.com

TABLE OF CONTENTS

IINTRODUCTION and A PHILADELPHIA EAGLE

"Pick the target, freeze it, personalize it, polarize it. Cut off the support network and and isolate the target from sympathy. Go after people and not institutions; people hurt faster than institutions. This is cruel, but very effective. Direct, personalized criticism and ridicule work." – Saul Alinsky

The title, "Tribe of Cannibals," refers to a quote from a Merck Manual published in the 1980s. In a chapter on mental health, Merck stated that the person who bucked the system, who went outside the tribal norms, so to speak, was the mentally ill party. That is to say, that the "vegetarian" in the tribe of cannibals was the crazy one, as opposed to the cannibals dying from kuru kuru, a cannibalism related motor neuron disease, similar to Bovine Spongiform Epilepsy (Mad Cow Disease) or Jacob Kreutzfeld Disease.

Such tribes are sadly analogous to the Democrat Party, cannibalizing their own country, cannibalizing the bodies of pre-natal babies for profit, destroying the professional lives of their opponents, while impugning the mental health of citizens invested in Faith, Family, Nation, the three pillars of good mental, physical and NATIONAL HEALTH – and the very survival of Homo Sapiens! Also demanding cult like conformity, like Facebook, as educated Conservatives have discovered to their horror.

I was outside the tribal norms of Roosevelt Island from day one. I was the Republican Pro-Lifer, outnumbered by "the tribe!" Of the rest, 98-99% were mostly connected to the Democrat Party in one way or another as the "bosses" from the Lenox HSill and East Harlem

Democrat Clubs or the minions, exchanging personal integrity for jobs for votes or housing for votes, or both. While the key players were lethal, the stupidity, conformity and lack of awareness of their "*Kool Aid*" drinking followers made them equally dangerous, because they were casually used to collect information, spy and report on their neighbors but without salary or benefit – the Useful Idiots!

Collectively, if you didn't "drink their Kool Aid," the Democrats would devour you, your hopes, your dreams, your aspirations, your work, the products and income from your work, and then spit you out through their fangs.

In other words, "cannibalize" the outsider. Why not? Through abortion profiteering, they cannibalize their own.

Too late, I realized that /was the "vegetarian" in a Tribe of Cannibals.

I was pro Life, outnumbered 5,000:1 by baby butchering neo communists.

They would take everything I owned, and then try to take my life, that of my children and my friends.

And there would be no recourse. While the NYPD "foot soldiers" remained honest and did not suffer from the dreaded "kuru kuru" of the mind, the NY and Brooklyn DA's office, the NYS AG Andrew Cuomo, the Governor of NYS past and present, the diktators (sic) at RIOC, Victims' Services and Judge Eileen Rakower along with any number of attorneys, all seemed afflicted by the same wasting, corrupting disease.

A disease that often preceded *extinction.*

Their minds had atrophied, their consciences unresponsive, their individuality. What remained was a zombie like lurch to greed and power, combined with a hatred of all that was pure, beautiful, dynamic, and above all, *innocent.*

Hence the rabid slaughter of the human prenatal baby in what was intended as the safest place for his or her protection and nourishment, the mother's womb.

"I had nothing really of my own to show…" Goethe's Mephistopheles

They had "nothing really of their own to show…"

A PHILADELPHIA EAGLE

On July 3rd, 2017, as I walked up a historical roadway or "Pike" toward a charming suburb of Philadelphia, I observed a house with an overgrown garden and an antique statue of a rather cheeky rat by the driveway.

I was pondering whether returning to the USA was, after all that was said and done, a good idea. The contents of this book will clarify that doubt.

As I passed the house, a giant American bald eagle landed in the trees beside me. From the corner of my eye I saw the white head, yellow beak, black talons and the general body, more or less camouflaged by the trees, of the iconic American bald eagle. Awesome and scary. Was I about to become "lunch?"

In the beautiful North West USA, as my son brought me on a farewell tour of the beautiful forests, glens, rivers of Washington State, an eagle suddenly sprung from hiding, soared upward toward us, and then crossed the ravine. We were standing in an elevated spot in a National Park…It was an enchanted moment.

Two years later, his East Coast cousin welcomed me home. It was the eve of July 4, 2016.

The following night was July Fourth, Independence Day. After years of abuse, harassment and violence from New York State and New York City rogue employees, I stopped going outside alone, unless accompanied by witness or protector. On Alinsky Island, the NY 10044 Gulag, I had to hire a bodyguard when my "buddyguard," Tom, an actor, was unavailable.

I believe the stress of that time, along with the toxic effects of 9/11 contributed to Tom's suffering and premature death. He died alone, hungry. His social worker assured me that he was cared for. He wasn't. No one called, no one cared, except the NY Surrogate's office when they saw an opportunity to plunder his belongings, even targeting his gravesite!

In Pennsylvania, however, the fireworks proved irresistible. I walked outside, near to WaWa – where there are always good people about and occasionally cops and a phone should any evil – or NYS vultures come a calling, and stood along the Pike where my ancestors walked so long ago to fight one of the definitive battles of the American Revolution, the Battle of Lafayette Hill.

I could imagine their response to the beauty of natural America and that many must have longed to remain in the USA, and bring their families from the cartel controlled, dark satanic mills in the smog-filled cities to the fertile beauty of the New World.

However, the mad King George, an apparent porphyriac, and tool of the Rothschild war brokers, would have punished their families severely should any soldier choose to break ranks, so they returned to wounded

England with their dreams of an unspoiled country and a new, unstriated life unfulfilled.

Poor King George, Hahnemann discovered the one remedy most likely to cure him only a few years after his painful death. In which case, the course of history might have altered drastically.

God did not favor him that way.

A breeze broke the dusk and softened the humidity as the pyrotechnics brightened the darkening sky.

For the first time since arriving in the USA, I felt safe to stand alone outside, day or night, and enjoy the simple pleasures of life, which are, after all, the greatest and most enduring – Liberty, the heritage of our extraordinary humanity, and witness to our God given Free Will and the Liberty guaranteed by the extraordinary men and women who founded "these here United States of America."

II

MEMORIAL WALL OF CHILDREN DEAD OR DAMAGED BY AND ON ROOSEVELT ISLAND

These are just the few kids of my acquaintance, whom I observed as they grew up on Isle of Woe. Most were very, very sweet kids. Parents were Democrats.

Sad to say, these children were not exceptions. I've listed those whose stories I know best, in the following list which applies to the original residents and merely reflected the outcome for most of the children on the island. Alinsky's "control the outcome." After the Section 8 building was constructed, Mrs V, an immigrant from Poland, saw her beautiful, blonde 12 year old daughter followed home every evening by a posse of "homeys" – black street thugs – and sent her back to Poland - to Boarding School.

Her boys already had a serious drug problem. One stopped the day he saw jets flying into the twin towers and joined the US Army.

Again, in bed with the Democrats. She worked for a very warped Judge.

Interestingly, when news of a new Section 8 building was announced, the liberals started to leave at the alleged rate of 400 families a month, hence the term NIMBY Liberals. Not in My Back Yard...

The Island and its ethos of drugs, abortion, minimal standards, promiscuity, etc., and no professional policing, no "guns," controlled by trumped up security guards with criminal records, and no accountability nor oversight, allowed a climate of gangsterism and fear to prevail. The loss of parental control via the "no borders" rat maze of apartment buildings didn't help; the ubiquitous CCTV cameras allowed for bullies and blackmailers but were surprisingly absent when evidence against the criminal "Public Safety" Gestapo was desperately needed.

Even worse, was the fact that when the children knew that their friends were being framed they were too frightened to inform the police or go against the town bullies. And so a teenager named L. Schwartz was jailed for a crime he did not commit – the baseball bat assault on Lyle, the assailant being Carlos Guzman, illegal immigrant from Columbia, who went on to attempt the life of a young GOP voter.

The white Christian kids of European extraction, especially the children of educated but naïve immigrants were the primary targets, but occasionally, the children of Jewish liberals got into harm's way, their parents' politics of denial making them vulnerable to strangers and other illegal aliens.

Note – legal immigrants are fingerprinted. Illegals are not. They produce no ID, no history, no reports, no references, but slip through the cracks and find their way to Isle of Woe.

DR = known substance abuser DRF = Drugs in family D = family committed Democrats ETOH = Alcoholism in family. A = known abortion in family, AP by parent, parents or AC child.

X, X   Two girls, 7 and 8 were abducted from the Roosevelt Island playground by a 14 year old with a history of child sexual abuse. He was a white kid living on the borderlands of the projects. He took them from the playground, up to the Motorgate building (parking) and across the bridge into Queens, *without any obstruction.* There was a manned "safety booth" at the entrance to the bridge but none of the Security detail took the slightest heed of the two little girls leaving the Island with the furtive teenager.

A police officer from Nassau Co passed them in Motorgate and did nothing. Of course it wasn't his jurisdiction, but those girls played with his daughters and were well known to him.

He was a heavy cocaine addict and island dealer.

Despite changing residence 12 times in three years, he passed the intense screening "required" for residents of that very "special" Island – by saying he was, wait for it, part native American!

CF   D DR DRF AP. Expelled from Kg age 6. (Developmentally delayed due to head trauma and gestational substance abuse.) Convicted of attempted murder by the infliction of multiple stab wounds in another 15 year old, a male. Served time; multiple arrests for breaking and entering, armed robbery, assault, etc. Charges always dropped, evidence suppressed. Dropout.

LG   DR DRF. Left school at 13, ran away with a rock star age 15. Dropout.

JM   Raped by 14 year old cousin when aged 8; at age 14 tried to rape an 8 year old boy. Mother knew but let him babysit my son. Island paediatrician knew. Baby faced psychopath.

DS   D DRF DR. Prolonged Juvenile detention upstate. Dropout. Member of gang whose initiation required new members to assault any white person on the head with a hammer.

JF   D DRF DR. Teens – convicted of heroin distribution and dealing

JF's gf. D DR. Anorectic, suicide. Teenager

CR   DR 15, Cocaine, drop out. Reclaimed life, did well. Humanitarian.

DR   D DRF. 14, 15 conviction for armed robbery with other island teens. HS Drop out

CC   D AC +AP. DROP OUT @ age 13, raped by uncle in law age 15, 4 abortions by age 19, under coercion by her father.

K boys   D AP DR. 13 – 15 One in rehab the other committed x 2 years in psyche unit.

SC   D AP. 20s convictions for drug and arms dealing. Raised on Gulag.

BJ   D DR DRF Obnoxious, street bully, probably served time, but no confirmation on that, protected by Public "Safety" thugs.
Harassed and bullied decent kids into joining graffiti gang. His father was Jeff Jones, Deacon at the Protestant Church and Director of RIOC's HR, i.e., Demrat Jobs for Votes and housing program, with RF.

JS D ETOH DR 15, found murdered under the 59th street bridge every bone in his body broken. Worse injuries than a jump or accidental "fall." Case still open. The illegal immigrant from Columbia who hacked open the head of another Island youth mentioned JS before producing a crowbar and machete and assaulting another Island teenager. JS was one of the island's many molested children. RIP.

X The teenager who jumped out of a third story window when RIPS appeared. Related to or connected with the Romanians. RIP.

XUs The many unknown teenagers who disappeared off the Island. Prime suspects are Cesar aka Wilson Toro (RIPS) Michelle Evans (RIPS) and EMS punks, Ruger and Fellaria.

AK Two years rehab. Framed by SC with apparent collusion of RIPS. AK's mother organised positively on behalf of the Eastwood tenants. SC contacted AK, arranged to meet. SC planted marijuana on AK, RIPS "suddenly" appeared out of nowhere, arrested only AK. RIHM told his mother that he would be imprisoned if she did not stop her tenant advocacy. To save (their) face, he would be sent to rehab. AK's mother was one of the few honourable people on the Gulag.

JM Father killed in Attica riots. He was reportedly a member of the Weathermen Underground, an associate of William Ayers et al. He was a difficult teenager, no sense of boundaries, became a porn producer. Mother was a "sweet" little Jewish woman.

On August 28, 2000, a Federal judge awarded $8 million to the survivors of the Attica riots. JM was awarded $25,000.

There was a variety of children from UN families, some allowed to run wild, some to physically and sexually assault their mothers in public; some were runaways, sleeping in the Eastwood basement. Some were sexual predators in their early teens, suggestive of previous early childhood sexual assault.

There were many such kids on the Island – from working families, from privileged families, from UN families, from some already deeply into the far left miserology; others, like us, Innocents Abroad. Post War Europe did not equip us for such insanity. It was too busy rebuilding with the certainty that such a war would never erupt again, but now that Europe has overtaken us in the conversion to Islamo-Communism, terrible wars rage on around the world. However, it still may be difficult, if not impossible, to understand the devastating consequences of life trapped in a totalitarian police state – 2 miles long x 600 yards wide – in the middle of the East River, both Jurisdictionally Manhattan and Queens, City and /or State, but neither. Inbuilt Alinsky KHAOS!

The Roosevelt Island Gulag was the experiment to de-Constitutionalise the USA.

No Stars and Stripes flew on Main Street for the first 10 years despite requests by at least one "Brit!"

No elected representatives. Yes, the Island was a feeder for votes for Rat candidates *representing other areas,* with NY 10044 as a tag along, but otherwise, a Gulag *intended as an experiment in rule by Corporation.* Rule by appointed rulers – a DICTATORSHIP, to be spread covertly across the entire USA.

No redress.

No real cops, but hey, happy people, RIPS don't have guns, we're safe – the delusions of liberalism.

There was *no redress* against abuses by the RIPS. They did not have the same controls as the *gentlemen* in the NYPD, nor any oversight whatsoever, outside of lawsuits. And they were careful to intimidate witnesses, lie to the NYPD and hide evidence, but "no guns," so they could assault and torment our children with impunity!

No free enterprise. Store fronts left unused for decades. Rented to foreigners, mostly, some suspected of money laundering. "One" of everything. No healthy competition allowed.

No Emergency or other medical services. Eventually a paediatrician and dentist, both "Party players," offered professional services, even as a very wealthy internist from the original NWO cadre, and co-publisher of the mysterious "Main Street Liar" decided to make House Calls on the Senior Citizens.

There is no longer a "Seniors" building, just high priced condos.

No Exit.

Enter George Soros and Move on dot org!

Every Saturday during election years, hobnobbing with Rat Party cohorts in the Trellis coffee shop.

The Good Shepherd Church used as a meeting place for Move on dot org's mobilisation of "campaigners" around the country.

The Good Shepherd Church used as a meeting place for the subversives in the RIOC diktat, a place where families were destroyed.

Beautiful building with 600 apartments in excellent condition, the "Nurses' Residence," allowed to decay and rot in order to obtain a demolition order – while there was a housing crisis in New York.

No provision made for emergency evacuations from the Island in case of terrorism or natural disaster. Dead sitting ducks. Geese. Ducks can count and protect their offspring. Abortion fanatics, well...they devour theirs...

III

SHIPWRECKED and MAROONED

<u>November 1976, my family moved into Roosevelt Island –
Siberia in the East River</u>

Personal Reference was from Ambassador Walter
Curley, Reagan Ambassador to France and Ford
Ambassador to Ireland.

Next door apartment was inhabited by R Fernandez, aka
RF or the thug.

RF was the "local co-ordinator for the Board of Elections
for the "Gulag," and a Lenox Hill DemocRat Party 'Officer.'
President of the 'Ladies (?!!) Auxiliary' allowed her to
push the Demrat Jobs for Votes at Goldwater Coler
Hospital as well as jobs for votes at Public Safety.

RF had access to Housing Records, through Thelma
McIntosh, another cohort.

She also appeared to have an 'apartments for votes'
system going, whereby Romanians and other East
Europeans could immediately bypass the two year
waiting lists and access apartments.

She took one look at my beautiful 'white male' baby and
declared war.

This war included:

Slander

Overt harassment and hostility.

Doors slammed in my face – Romanians 'sicced' on me
when I went into the laundry room, etc.

Calling up work places, calling me a racist, etc. *All that time me and my children were the victim of intense racism.*

Ensuring that my checks were mislaid at Coler Hospital through her cronies.

Organising a smear campaign against me when I was nominated to Governor Pataki's RIOC Board. Kept the calls going to his office accusing me of "racism." The man who nominated me was black, for Heaven's sake – Dr. Jerome Blue, a gentleman. *The NY Rats took him down too!*

Threatening me.

Threats were followed by attempts on my son's life – after a proposal submitted *at the request of the Medical Director at Goldwater* passed seven committees, and was about to receive a grant from NYU. The proposal was later modified and someone else received the grant.

Threats were followed by attempts on my life by Public Safety THUGS – also in her 'pay' as part of the Rat Party jobs for votes programs.

In this she had the collusion of Jeff Jones, among others.

In other words, through the Democrat Club at Lenox Hill, this semi-literate monster, wielded enough influence to spy on, follow, harass, slander me and my family, bring false charges against my son and literally wage war on me and my family for decades, and sabotage every opportunity that I created or slam shut every door my dear friend, Fred Von Stange, of the USIS, tried to open for me to get out of that toxic, obnoxious environment.

I have a rare anemia which limited my stamina. I would and have thrived elsewhere, but Roosevelt Island was a killer in more ways than one. It was only through God's grace that I survived any of it, but it is a shame and disgrace on the USA that such a vile, prolonged and intense violation of my and my family's Civil Liberties and Human Rights were allowed to continue for decades.

And that so many innocents remain on the NYPD 114th books as "cold cases."

IV

<u>THE ROAD TO HELLTOWN 10044</u>

Or what brought me to the Isle of Woe!

Designed by the Frankfurt School of Marxism, i.e., Columbia U School of Sociology, conjoined with the "usual suspects," and built on Alinsky principles of control through chaos and disinformation, Roosevelt Island appeared and still appears to be the prototype for the "conversion" of the USA from a Constitutional Republic to a Corporate entity, where the Residents are mostly reduced to the status of "minions."

It is no coincidence that *during the Obama years* the image of a "minion" was artificially engineered by Hollywood from the servile "Renfield Spiders" to the cute little yellow cartoon characters now beloved of children.

It is no coincidence that Hillary Clinton declared her candidacy for the Presidency of the USA on Roosevelt Island, nor that George Soros was a regular visitor there during election years, nor that Move on.org appeared to have its NY headquarters there, and that the Good Shepherd Church building cum Community Center was used to recruit "campaigners" to travel to other States during the Obama campaign, campaigners definitely, voters probably~

It is no coincidence that there were no legitimate police in the Gulag, just a bunch of Bolshevik, criminal thugs, and while the "useful idiots" on Roosevelt Island prided themselves on the absence of guns, the Gulag Gestapo were battering their children, putting them under false arrest, false charges, all the while allowing predators and dealers to also poison, corrupt and abuse their children. But they didn't carry guns, oh goody goody!

Another illusion, like the electric buses that kept breaking down, and the tramway that kept shutting down, was that it was "the safest place in New York!"

In most areas of Manhattan you could walk pretty safely until near to midnight. On the Gulag the gangs took over the North East side of the street at 7.00pm, with full collusion of "Public Safety," and made it a no go area, if you were alone and unaccompanied.

There were no health services on the Island, aside from the Residential Hospitals, which served their own patients and used Bellevue's ER services when necessary.

Heather, a retired army nurse, ex 'Nam, took care of most emergencies, voluntarily and out of the goodness of her heart – but that was not part of the "Khaos" program. She was told to cease and desist.

Medical services were unavailable on the Gulag, increasing the risk of fatalities, even as residents leapt from windows, and the Roosevelt Island bridge was used as a suicide launching pad – all covered up - and children were raped in the schools and abducted from the playgrounds, and Roosevelt Island Public Safety, harassed, hounded, hunted, stalked, battered, physically and sexually abused children and youth and allowed the children of the infamous Roosevelt Island Operating Corporation to batter other children and teenagers, and arrested the children of Conservative pro-Lifers on false charges, or other children and youth in order to protect their favorites – which just happened to be Hispanic illegal aliens, protected by the Democrat Party.

One side of the Island was "normal," mostly foreigners, mostly UN people freeloading on the Mitchel Lama 226 Subsidies to which they were *not* entitled. UN professionals already receive hefty housing and other subsidies thanks to the generosity of the American taxpayer. This was blatant double dipping, but even more significant, as I later explore, was the fact that most of the Third World and left wing Europeans, along with any number of criminals, seemed to know all about the Gulag, whereas the Americans, whose tax dollars paid for it, had never heard of it.

Even Vatican banker hid out there prior to returning to London, most likely lured by assurances of safety. He "hanged himself" from Waterloo Bridge. Right, and witnesses against Hillary Clinton really did shoot themselves in the back of the head.

Most of the "foreigners," i.e. "visitors" or temporary residents seemed somewhat contemptuous of America's Liberties. Most wanted to stay on after their official posting was fulfilled.

New York Democrats knew of the "Gulag," but do they classify as "Americans" or as "Bolshevik nation!"

How many were involved and to which levels in that corrupted proto Communist Party? _After an Iranian named Ari Kalimian destroyed our old but sound apartment in Manhattan, turning off heat and hot water every Friday to Monday for years, summer and winter alike, we moved to a smaller apartment in Manhattan, also in an older building.

However, as major construction was in progress nearby, we were frequently invaded by nasty rodents, which have come to symbolize the RAT Party to me. I sat up every night on the sofa bed with my 4 year old daughter on one side and my son on the other while my poor late husband, an actor, slept in the tiny spare room. Where were the

"Beautiful for Spacious Skies?" Not on 73rd Street! Not on the Democrat Party monopolized Upper East Side!

In all my growing years in Europe, I never anticipated such experiences in the USA, despite being raised in a left wing household on terms like "American imperialism," "British Imperialism," "Opiate of the people," and "you have to kill your mother for the good of the people," and being fed books like "The Urban Jungle," "The Ragged Trousered Philanthropists" and such. As far as I knew, those books were historical! Until I met Fr Cosgrave, SJ, who had the Bolshevik infiltration of the USA – infiltrating as refugees no less – tabbed and recorded to a "t," I was baffled, confused and dismayed by my experiences in the "greatest city in the world!" I was shocked at the level of Communist infiltration and ideology in the USA.

I had left mega opportunities in the UK, ROI and Italy, to be reduced to "Irish Immigrant" in a nation that proclaims equality.

Then again, are NYC, Chicago, Olympia and Albany (NYS) really the USA – or outposts of Soviet era Moscow and Frankfurt, the heart and home of Communism transplanted in the USA since the Bolshevik saboteurs infiltrated the refugee camps and brought their agit prop to the free and fair United States!

Roosevelt Island certainly was as "red" as the color of the tram, as red as its name, as red as the star on the Chi-Com flag, as blood-red as the flag of the USSR, as red as the now scarlet Harvard, and as red as the Rot on the shield of Adam Bauer Rothschild, goldsmith, banker, briber and creator of the new economic "Imperialism" – world domination through control of the ebb and flow of the world!

FDNY wanted one of the aerial tramway cabins painted blue – which made sense for rapid emergency identification, and what a furore that caused. Same when they painted the Roosevelt Island Bridge another color.

Nothing doing! The Island was red and the committed islanders "red" to the core.

They were anti American subversives in every sense of the word, and at almost every level.

Without the corruption in the Demo'Rat Party, Kalimian would have been shut down and our Manhattan apartment maintained. In fact, Kalimian should have been deported for what he did to Americans, and may still continue to do now that his pit bull lawyer, Sabrina Kraus, is a Judge on Housing Court.

I later discovered that an elderly patient of mine and resident in a Kalimian building was constantly scoffed at for complaining about the cold and shown a toy thermostat, fixed at 78F. Ari Kalimian was notorious for that, now he has a crony in the court.

God help New Yorkers in trouble!

An encounter with a nice *German* lady in a pediatrician's office led to a visit to Looney Toon's Island.

And a two year lease led to a lifetime of entrapment.

Sartre's Hell had no comparison with that Isle of Woe, Isle of Doom, the New York Gulag 10044 and it's Tribe of Cannibals. The play "No Exit" expresses Hell as an eternal dinner party with the same excruciatingly boring and annoying people. These were worse than boring. They were so stupid, that even though they wanted rid of the pro-Life Conservatives, they sabotaged every effort to leave!

There was no exit, no escape from the Gulag. It was like *living* on the set of "The Prisoner." Every path out brought us right back into the man-made Alinsky Hell. Ultimately, I believe that the Lord allowed that for very good reason. Unless you had been raised in far left ideology, and knew the "playbook" it would be easy to lose faith in one's own perceptions. Indeed many ended up with nervous break-downs, and on medication. They were told, by the Rat Party and the Media that the Gulag was "Paradise Island," therefore any negativity had to be from the individual, and so the dichotomy between the *enforced* or planted perception and the *reality* of life on "Helltown" led to intense cognitive dissonance, one that found no respect within the confines of the island or interest outside it. For all intents and purposes, we were marooned and isolated, just not allowed to believe it.

Sartre's "No Exit" had to be the inspiration for the lack of decent transportation on and off the Island; for the deliberate confusion re train schedules and subway service to the Gulag. It was relatively easy to know which train to take to Manhattan – there was only one and if you stood on the right platform – there were only two – in the deepest, subterranean, below sea level subway station in NY, if not the world, you just took the first train that came along. Of course, you might have to dodge the anti-white racists, the UN sleaze merchants, the congenital whiners, etc., but at least you knew the next station was just a few minutes away.

The next station being 63rd and Lexington, *the* meeting point for Afghan, Bengali and Pakistani cab drivers, where they changed shifts. One man, I am certain, was a young Bowe Bergdahl, blonde, bland and bearded, anxiously seeking directions for the side roads to Peshawar. I played "nosy lady" – one look at the guy told me that a few screws were missing and that the fair young

American hitch-hiking to Peshawar alone, as a civilian, would never return alive. He was very intense, slight in appearance, but fit. He eventually left without ascertaining "safest routes to hitch hike to Peshawar," but eventually turned up on the evening news in a US Army uniform!

It is very painful to consider, that, if I had ignored him, five heroic soldiers would still be alive.

Slight diversion there. The return journey to the Gulag was always a nightmare, especially if you were returning from a "hub" with multiple trains. The MTA would frequently switch services to the Gulag, so that it was all but impossible to ascertain whether the R, Q, N, 7 / whatever, train would take you back there after dark. We could end up in Brooklyn, or at JFK, or Harlem. Gradually we stopped attending opera, ballet, theatre, lectures. The stench of urine at the Metropolitan Opera stations (Lincoln Center) was bad enough, but...the confusion was unbearable.

For a few years, the Q train was assigned to the Island, and worked well. Just when we were feeling safe, they switched it again to the "either or" – "guess which train takes you back..."

Alinsky rules! The Island of the demon "Khaos," a word "scratchitti'ed" on the trains by the son of the HR Director, and town bully.

No doubt in my mind that Hillary Clinton's mentor and idol, Saul Alinsky, the promotor of misery, was, indeed, a "luciferian."

"Khaos" ruled that particular Circle of Hell.

V

OPERATION VOTE RIGGING

Jobs for votes were operated by the local co-ordinator for the Board of Elections. She was an officer of the Lenox Hill Democrat Club running the "jobs for votes" line in the Coler and Goldwater Hospitals, through her position as head of the "Ladies Auxiliary." West Indian accents were omnipresent in the LPN changing room! She also had the "jobs for votes" line on Public Safety and RIHM due to her influence with the Jeff and Nicky Jones, Jeff being the HR Director of RIOC, all connected with either Lenox Hill Democrat Clubs or East Harlem, or both!

Her name was Roslyn Fernandez. Like former US AG Eric Holder's family, she was from Barbados, and was doubtless acquainted, if not actually related. She once loaded torpedoes into shells, a precursor to her lethal work with the Demo'rat party. The polite term for her was "The Enforcer." Her manner was so aggressive that others called her "the silverback." I occasionally refer to her as that, as I do Angela Merkel, a white German Communist who adopts gorilla like poses when speaking "at" our President Trump.

Tangentially, it has been alleged that Holder was a domestic terrorist. He with his fellow black moslems took over an ROTC centre in Columbia U in 1973 and occupied it for a week. They were armed – and not with sheets and pillows. You don't take over a military training centre with sheets and pillows. Sorry, Snopes, that just doesn't wash!

Despite having participated in another armed occupation of a faculty office that of Dean Coleman, Coleman wrote Holder's recommendation to Columbia Law!

It's also interesting that Holder admitted to never doing an exam until his junior year as the black students always managed to hold a protest or "strike" at exam time.

Wonder if the white students ever thought of that. In Holder's own words...

"I did not take a final exam until my junior year at Columbia — we were on strike every time finals seemed to roll around — but we ran out of issues by that third year.

I also recall one day when we got together and decided to peacefully occupy one of the campus offices. We felt passionately about the need for a place where black students could gather and we went ahead and staged our sit-in. This became the black student's lounge <u>in what was then Hartley Hall</u>. The person who we had to negotiate with, and whose office we also occupied later, was Dean Henry Coleman. In the ultimate display of chutzpah I later asked Dean Coleman to write my law school recommendations. This being Columbia of course he agreed. He was a great, generous man. This College allowed an impetuous, testosterone laced youngster to *express himself in ways that other institutions would have considered unacceptable. Not Columbia. This is why I love this place.*" (The italics are mine.)

And yes, Columbia U's former Drama Professor had no scruples about stealing the concepts and work of a brilliant young dramatist and trying to seduce his friend's wife. Ugh! Sleaze on steroid!

And there we have Columbia U again! Holder, Obama, Soros, Move on.org Lenox Hill Democrat Club, East Harlem Democrats, Columbia U, all linked to a tiny Island in the middle of the East River, an Island under the control of a semi literate thug and former munitions worker aka RF.

She was a large, mannish woman with a belligerent manner and a racist attitude to white Americans. She hated Republicans with a vengeance. It was a tragedy for us that we were offered the apartment next door to her and her drug addicted prostituted daughter and brain damaged granddaughter. Innocents led to the slaughter! Instinct said to ask to see another one, but Dermot, being an actor and Irish just wanted to get the whole thing over with, so with a really bad feeling on my part, we moved in.

She was semi-literate and left a note under our door the night we moved in. Written in pencil and crudely spelled, the message was loud and clear: "You are not wanted here."

For starters, she was no "lady," and secondly, she did no charity work with the patients, just found when jobs were available and placed her candidates in the line-up. Same with the housing for votes. Who could object to a "churchgoing" black lady, especially one sleeping with the Reverend every Friday! All were afraid to say anything against her. The obvious response would be "you must be a racist...!"

Public Safety were hired through RIOC. RIOC's head of Human Resources liaised with the Enforcer. All were pre-acquainted through the Lenox Hill Democrat Club and the East Harlem Democrat Club.

While RF was attempting to destroy my family, she lost two daughters, first one to AIDS, and then another, a diabetic.

Historically, it may be of interest that Bill Clinton planted his post Presidential HQ in East Harlem, i.e., 125th Street, and Hitlery launched her disastrous 2016 Presidential campaign from Alinsky Island.

The name of the first head of Human Resources for the dictatorship called RIOC was Jeff Jones. He was married to Nikki Jones, a black woman with a long, artificial braid down her back, who claimed her "freckles" were from an Irish plantation overseer who raped her ancestors.

Nothing racist there!

The reality, according to Molly O'Rourke, former food columnist for the NY Times Magazine, was that the first wave of pre Famine Irish immigrants was mostly male. They *married* blacks and Chinese. For black women, marriage was so important for their social hierarchies that up to the third millennium that once a friend was married they referred to one another as "Mrs," followed by the surname of her husband. It was a sign of respect to be called "Mrs." Feminism took care of that.

That article was more or less the last we heard from Molly! She was quickly dropped from the NY Times Sunday Magazine section.

It does however explain an almost demonic hatred of white Irish females, both young and mature who started immigrating during and after the Famine. As it was natural to gravitate to their own, Irish men married Irish girls and opportunities for marital status among the Americans of African heritage diminished.

Unnerved by the possibility of former slaves converting to Catholicism through marriage to Irish Catholics, the Protestant churches stepped up, recruiting and nurturing black congregants and refusing to condemn the various "Know Nothings" and other vituperative groups spraying hatred toward the Irish in general and Catholicism in particular.

It is interesting to note that the renovated Ellis Island Museum shows none of the hardships experienced by the European Immigrants who built the USA, and has all but completely destroyed the Irish Exhibits which once spread through three massive rooms, but are now barely visible on one wall, shared by a few other "insignificant" ethnic groups, i.e., white Christian Europeans. A symbolic GENOCIDE of America's Euro-Christian heritage.

In that light, also, is the fact that before I spoke up, the East Side Tenement Museum had a "room" representing every immigrant ethnic group – except, of course, the Irish.

They have an "Irish Room" now. I note that I was not invited to the opening, even though it was my input and impetus that brought it about, and that the Director gave my play to an amateur to dispose of.

Good or lousy, an original drama is the literary PROPERTY of the dramatists. Mine are certainly of value, some were definitely ahead of their time, many on terrorism. But they cannot be passed around without permission of the dramatist. That is unlawful and THEFT.

It is one matter when such prejudices are inchoate and sporadic. I unwittingly brought my children to an environment that was ultra-Liberal, proto Communist, virulently anti-Catholic, and definitely Hibernophobic – Marcuse's divided and weaponised society.

Nikki Jones' husband, Jeff Jones, was the head of Human Resources at RIOC, a Deacon at the mixed denomination Protestant Church, and completely henpecked by his wife. He was white.

Protected by her husband's status as a RIOC apparatchik, and her friend, RF's position in the Rat Party, Mrs. Jones ran an illegal day care centre from her apartment. In poor health at the time, I foolishly signed my son up, as there were no legit organised amenities at the time. Three days later, I watched from the window as she pushed my sweet little two year old boy away from her. When I clambered down the stairs, ran down the ramp and around the corner to the river bench and confronted her, she boldly denied it.

That's a Democrat.

Jeff Jones also hired his teenage daughter to work as a tramway attendant at the optimum salary with full benefits not offered to permanent workers, even nepotistic friends. In the early 1980s Jessica Jones received $14.00 per hour start up with full benefits and vacation.

The job of tramway operator is simple enough when things are going well, but if not, lives can be at risk. The vacuous teenager with a personal hair fetish was neither interested nor capable of identifying or dealing with any serious or moderate difficulty or incident.

And so Operation Corrupting America was well under way at Roosevelt Island Operating Corp from the very beginning.

The Jones' mixed race son was Benjamin, a discontented, obese bully, who was ignored by his mother as she tended to almost every other child, for money, of course. He was two years older than my son, six inches taller at the time and three times his weight, conservatively speaking.

Unknown to his father, but with the consent and support of Roosevelt Island Public "Safety," Benjamin became the Main Street bully, the graffiti gang organiser, and if you're so misfortunate as to use the NY subway system, you may still see his scratchitti "handle" on the window of an NY subway train.

True to the Alinsky influence, his "handle" was "KHAOS," the demon that controlled that island!

In his teens, Benjamin Jones became the three hundred pound bully who bit my son's leg, pounded his head into the sidewalk, and then went whining to his father when my 180lb, 2 year younger son, knocked him to the ground. *This assault against my son took place in the presence of and under the sneering gaze of the perverts at Roosevelt Island Public Safety. They took no action against Jeff Jones' son despite imminent danger to my younger, lighter, sensitive son. The "hit" was in play.*

After a one on one with his father, during which I quietly elucidated the truth about Benjamin, Jeff Jones and his family left town. Jeff suddenly developed Multiple Sclerosis and was last seen by me being wheeled by his "loving wife" Nikki shortly before he died.

Addendum: Mixed race children on the Gulag were more often children of single white mothers and abandoning black fathers. The "zeitgeist" of the white bashing era was to force mixed race children to choose just one heritage. As all the government grants and privileges went to black kids, and black culture was hyper-promoted, they would opt for their black heritage. This was incredibly cruel, as they had to then deny and reject the white mothers who nurtured them, thereby setting up internal conflicts, almost impossible to resolve without professional assistance – and when the professionals were also PC liberals, what chance did they have, other than to turn to drugs, identity politics or "take a knee" against the nation and parent that nurtured them, irrespective of skin colour.

The "Khaos" identity denial program is in full swing now, no longer targeting race but gender identity, and attempting to destroy yet another generation.

From the tragic appearance of the "snowflakes," "Useful Idiots" recruited from colleges – another form of dependency culture – that part of the TAKEDOWN AMERICA Program appears effective.

From one of the innocents, lured and entrapped there:

"In trying to resolve the cognitive dissonance between enjoying life on Roosevelt Island and being governed by a monarch I have come to the realisation that voicing my concern over the primary manifestation of totalitarianism is mandatory. That is we have a "police" force (Public Safety) that is unchecked and ruled only by the king of the Island, the head of RIOC."

(Quotes on "police" are mine, and the Island was ruled covertly by George Soros. RIOC was an assembly of Yes men and women, political appointees)

"Over the past year, I have heard dozens of shocking circumstances in which Public Safety behaved atrociously: I hear of minors being arrested and harassed; people being ticketed for taking pictures of scenery; and of Public Safety acting as prosecutor judge and jury outside of the auspices of their responsibilities. Less importantly I have personally grown weary of being leered at as I walk to and from the train station before and after work..."

Hal Warsham, Letters, the Main Street WIRE Dec 20, 2008

Hal Warsham was new to the Island at the time, as yet, unaware that the leering is as sinister as the rest of the abuses listed in his excellent letter to the self-serving and compromised editor and publisher.

RIPS protected criminals and the youth knew it. It is no credit to the children of liberals that they allowed a teenager to be unjustly charged with a violent crime because they were afraid of the illegal Columbian who committed it and knew the anti-white racists at "Public Safety" would protect him.

The same Columbian who was released on his own recognisance right after slashing at my son with a machete.

I believe the teenager's name was Louis Schwartz.

Similarly, just before the assault on my son – which was preceded by a blow to the head with a tire iron – said Columbian started talking wildly about Jesse Sanabria, a 15 year old, troubled but fundamentally sweet youth, found at the base of the 59th Street Bridge with *every bone on his body broken.* Every single bone.

Still an open case, last I heard.

And then there was Anna (Finola) Bourke missing from her room at Coler for two weeks, found at the bottom of a stairwell.

RF knew that Finola was a friend of mine, and that Jesse's mother worked for me. As established she had a lot of clout in the Hospitals – and with the illegal aliens!

RF had plenty of connections at Coler Hospital, connections who would sneak into the Protestant Chapel and turn the organ back on after I had turned it off, in order for Chapin to fire me.

I then used the "Foreign Office" strategy of asking the Associate Chaplains to witness me turning it off. They were supportive and glad to do it.

They were both good people, one a "reformed" actor, and the other an AME Minister, who was not a racist and not a fan of RF's hostile and criminal behaviour. I liked them both, a lot.

The AME Minister was a perceptive woman and knew better than to confront RF on my behalf, nor did I want her to.

The primary suspect in the "case of the organ switch off" – Gladys – obtained a transfer out of the hospital into an apartment on the island in the Seniors /Disabled building.

Not a bad trade-off for a few seconds work of spying and sabotage every week, but she had lived in the hospital since childhood, so *faute de mieux.*

I'm glad she got a reprieve and a taste of freedom.

VI

NO EXIT– *Lasciate ogni speranza, voi ch'entrate*

Dante's 9th Circle of Hell! Due to the configuration of the Island and the bizarre, unhealthy and arduous lack of resources,ie, one supermarket, one deli, one pizzeria, one pharmacy, etc., I had to ration every gram of energy. My once recovered immune system kept crashing under the stress of life there, and between health crashes and tramway shutdowns and the horrendous, torturous, spine-torqueing, mini-bus ride, and unavailability of life generating Homeopathic remedies at the time, one activity after another folded, including professional opportunities, aided and abetted by direct sabotage from the hostiles, i.e. the Lenox Hill and East Harlem Democrats.

How could you build respect if you could not keep appointments? Unpunctuality is "kiss of death" fatal in New York, but also "crippling" in other professional areas.

For the non-"bankers" the tram just shut down at 10am, leaving us stranded. There was never any notification for the wildcat shut downs, e.g., an orange flag outside Public Safety. They later provided those for the *scheduled* shut downs, for which we already had advance notice.

I would allow an hour for a thirty minute journey only to arrive at the tram to discover it had arbitrarily shut down. Alternative transport usually took two uncomfortable hours.

This occurrence was so coincidental with my professional appointments, that I started to wonder if

"RF" had a hand in it. Certainly through the other "Dem'rat heroine," Louisa Jordan, she did have a direct connection to the Tram Director Paul Jordan. It was difficult, however, to understand a professional, to whom the State had entrusted the lives of thousands of Gulag residents, indulging in such petty games.

But were they petty?

Or were they strategic? To control the lives of the residents, surreptitiously turning up the heat as we grew increasingly aware and mystified at the lack of normalcy and the bizarre decisions of the "Government by Corporation," i.e. the unelected, often mysterious, unchallengeable, secretive, immutable "Komsomol"/diktat aka the Roosevelt Island Operating Corporation, limiting the power of the independent professionals?

Did they need us as a "control" group; antagonists to whom they could play "Planet of the Apes" games – i.e., pursuing, harassing, diminishing, shutting down? Or was R

F so mind numbingly stupid that she couldn't put one and one together and make two – i.e. that her attempts to drive us away, by destroying my career opportunities, only held me on that wretched Gulag / Isle of Woe decades longer than I originally intended.

To normal folk that might seem far-fetched, but after living in that "minimum security prison" (controlling / imprisoning through fear, etc.) I have come to realise the power of ignorance when combined with HATE.

Yes, there was a bus service, but that could take two hours to Manhattan depending on connections and whether it circled Cooler or Goldwater Hospital first.

That also had its hazards, such as a 300 lb Nurse's Aid from Coler Hospital sitting on my knee in order to try to force me to give my seat to her.

The driver was silent, the passengers were silent. I had to deal with her alone, and eventually threatened to charge her with assault, so after a few curses she stood up. On exiting the Q32, passengers came up and said well done, etc., but I lost respect for them. They witnessed an indignity, an assault, and remained silent. Cowards. New York is full of bullies and cowards – same coin, different sides, and they all vote Democrat.

I have had several encounters on the tram, and believe one was with the Central Park murderer – tram operator called the NYPD but RIPS got there first and diminished my credibility to the NYPD. They did take his name, and it was on the anniversary of the murder of a beautiful young actress, so if Cold Cases are interested they can tally the news account commemorating the anniversary (NY Post I believe) and perhaps, at least find a name in their records. There is more information if they want it.

The tram and bus was a Sartre-ian Hell. A small tin box, very uncomfortable, limited seating, originally designed for vacation goers and strong, well clad, muscled skiers, it was put into use as a commuter vessel that was useless in high winds, useless in lightning, constantly out of service – for hours, days, weeks, months even.

When down for months, the red buses, again designed for short rural hops, with minimal suspension, were put into service on New York's pot holed roads. My spine twinges at the memory of the drives over two bumpy bridges, and the long waits, standing at the freezing, unsheltered bus stops, waiting for one to show up.

The subway was often down too, and played "alphabet" trains at the week-end, so you were never sure which train to take when returning from a function. I stopped going to Opera, Theatre, and the Ballet, because I was terrified of ending up in some God forsaken area of Queens, Harlem, Manhattan, and the Bronx at midnight…

On one occasion I was on route to a function at City Hall as the guest of the City Council President, Christine Quinn. Before her election she was instrumental in saving the Hospital Chaplaincies - after I pointed out their services included patients with AIDs. Her then boss, Tom assigned her to that role, and she included me on her guest list on other occasions, despite me being a "Straight, white Catholic."

Taxis were "fun" too, once the moslems bought out the indigenous NY cabbies. Once I had to hop out at a red light and flee because the driver was speeding toward the Triborough Bridge, far, far out of my way. Threats, insults, attempts at recruitment, anti-American rhetoric were also common. I also noted that on the rare occasion a Roosevelt Islander offered to share a cab with me, they always stiffed on the tip – these would be the co-op owners, i.e. Democrat donors or their children.

Back to the tram. No escape! For five to ten minutes I was stuck with a gaggle of liberals, a "murder" of pro-abortion Democrats, dangerous as angry crows, but without the intelligence! If they had a problem, they would not hesitate to inflict it on me for the journey. If I were dressed up for an occasion, I was suddenly the most popular person in the tram – persons who avoided me like the plague would tell me how well I looked and ask where I going. And the crazies were out there too – another 300 lb black woman wanted to take up three spaces on the limited bench and tried to bully me into giving up my seat.

They all think they're "Rosa Parks," except they were clueless about her action and motivation.

She just sat in a front seat. She didn't displace anybody! But hey, why learn your own history when ignorance allows you to be a bully.

On another occasion I had to persuade the tram operators that the disabled could not generate heat when forced to wait on a high windy platform in 8F weather for an hour and were at severe risk of hypothermia.

They managed to get the little "pencil box" working very quickly to allow the disabled a safe return to the Gulag. Along with myself. Helping others really helps you help yourself!

Such were the joys of daily life on Alinsky Island. If the tram was functioning it was misery. If not, even more misery.

My health broke down, time and time again, and as I struggled to write, to produce, to practice, to take care of my family, and I succumbed to frequent bouts of pneumonia.

Storefronts were left open and unrented, losing revenue supposedly destined for the well- being and improvements of Loony Toons Island.

The Supermarket was rented to John Catsimatides, for $1.00 i.e., *one dollar,* per year. His food prices were the highest, his quality the lowest. Catsimatides bragged of donating $100,000 to Hillary Clinton's Senate Campaign.

No collusion there.

The Seniors had to be transported off Island to shop every week in order to buy affordable food and avoid malnutrition. I helped there, anonymously.

The Chinese were allowed to open a restaurant; the Greeks, a coffee shop; a Korean nail salon owner and fundraiser for North Korea who employed illegal Nepalese in her Salon, asked me how to generate business.

I replied, rather facetiously, to put a photo of the Clintons where passers-by could see it. Within a week the salon was rocking. Needless to say, the Commie sympathiser never said thank you or offered a courtesy manicure, but never failed to consult me on some problem or the other every time I stopped in for paid services.

As soon as another salon opened up I took my business there.

The Romanian flower shop was also mysterious, and generally assumed to be a money laundering outfit because most of the business appeared to be from off Islanders ordering flowers for the hospital residents – or for the rare funerals on the Island.

Very seldom did we see weddings, or baptisms in that abortion capital of Hell.

The first store on Looney Island was the Liquor Store – founded by Archie Seale's father, who was announced as the Mayor of the Island, without any election.

The communists in control were "amused." The normal people, "bemused!"

I liked Archie. He had integrity, and even though he was the leader of the Rainbow Coalition on the Isle of Woe, he stood up to me when Demonrat Koko, "Co-ordinator for the Board of Elections," falsely accused me of campaigning too close to the polling booth. Archie told the police that she was lying. I will always respect and appreciate him for that.

Did they need us as a "control" group; antagonists to whom they could play "Planet of the Apes" games – i.e., pursuing, harassing, diminishing, shutting down? Or was Koko so mind numbingly stupid that she couldn't put one and one together and make two – i.e. that her attempts to drive us away, by destroying my career opportunities, only held me on that wretched Gulag / Isle of Woe decades longer than I originally intended.

To normal folk that might seem far-fetched, but after living in that "minimum security prison" controlled and "imprisoned" through fear, etc., I have come to realise the power of ignorance when combined with HATE.

Yes, there was a bus service seat by her.

The driver was silent, the passengers were silent. I had to deal with her alone, and eventually threatened to charge her with assault, so after a few curses she stood up. On exiting the Q32, passengers came up and said well done, etc., but I lost respect for them. They witnessed an indignity, an assault, and remained silent. Cowards. New York is full of bullies and cowards – same coin, different sides, and they all vote Democrat.

"Lasciate ogni speranza, voi ch'entrate" – could Dante's 9th circle of Hell be worse than the Roosevelt Island Gulag?

How I longed for the Norfolk Broads of England, the beaches of Bournemouth, the New Forest, and La Scala Milan.

Despite terrible, chronic homesickness, I sensed that outside the Gulag, the 9th Circle of New York Hell, there was something magnificent about America.

And for that much credit goes to my dear, late friend, Fred Von Stange, of the USIS.

He tried so hard to get us off the Island, knew something was terribly wrong there, but no one could imagine the scale and depth of the infamy of the parties committed to the overthrow of America.

Soros was there. Move on.org creeps were there. The island was designed for Khaos and Kontrol, aided and abetted by all the usual suspects, the front page tyrants.

VII

UNUSUAL SUSPECT – JUSTICE DENIED.

It was either July or August of 2006, when, on route to the dreaded subway, I encountered a tall figure in a burqa. The figure sat, alone, on the edge of a sandpit, in a disused playground, staring straight ahead, but as I approached, the eyes were cast downward.

Although the playground was under repair, I am instinctively protective of children, and walked around this figure trying to ascertain some clue as to whether the creature was male or female, and whether it was 'scoping' the playground for future assault on a child.

I made "it" nervous. At one point it stood up, and it was clear that the body was that of a male, tall, skinny. Everything was covered except for the eyes, which remained downcast. The person clearly did not want to be identified.

However, as I stood, observing, wondering whether to say "hello" in Arabic, the left hand emerged, and moved in a slow, menacing manner in my direction.

Thirty years of Classical Ballet, studying movement, and how to express and interpret emotions through movement, said "loud and clear" to get the blazes out of there. It was a killer's hand! A premeditated, calculated killer's hand. It was *café au lait*, light brown, not white, with a tan; very smooth - not the muscled hand of a blue collar worker, and *menacing.*

I saw the same hand on television a year or so later, taking a tea cup from a silver tray. There is no doubt in my mind that was that of a well-known political figure who arrived on the Gulag to collect a "daughter" prior to a pivotal election, a little girl kept apart from the other children, never participating in public celebrations for the Island kiddies.

Not long after that, on or about August 6, 2006, an Emirates "Dreamliner" jet landed at JFK. This would have picked up journos, producers, publishers, politicians, donors and such for a free junket or jaunt to Dubai, the mouse-trap for ambitious westerners. Everything licit would be supplied, and possibly a few "illicit" items as well.

It is completely conceivable that Barack Obama would be on that junket and, after the media was wined and dined and coked up, be introduced as "The Next President of the United States of America!"

The August date provided just enough "lede" time for Time Magazine to place him on the October 23rd, 2006 cover, as "This could be the next President of the United States," – allowing a few weeks to *subliminally* influence undecided voters during the distractions of Hallowe'en, Thanksgiving and Christmas.

Diabolically clever. I often wonder if the previous and following encounters were related. They occurred shortly after the playground encounter.

On August 16th 2006 I took a break from a novel that I was writing on global terrorism, linking the threads together, and went for a walk.

Neil Jordan's crew had been on the Gulag for a couple of weeks, shooting The Brave One, so I expected to be safe. The presence of abundant outside witnesses served to inhibit the abuses of Roosevelt Island Gestapo aka Public Safety, who followed, stalked, harassed, threatened, attempted to intimidate me and my son for years, finally escalating to criminal violence in 2006.

My son was too frightened to report that RIPS had been physically and violently abusing him for over a decade, and allowing the pig ignorant children of RIOC executives, in particular, Ben Jones, son of Jeff Jones, to do likewise. "Roosevelt Island Public Safety" needs to be investigated and categorized as domestic terrorists. Andrew Cuomo needs a RICO investigation for collusion in their activities while he was Attorney General of New York, until and up to his present capacity as Governor.

My video testimony was played to Congress by William Windsor in February 2013. Lawless America, 984.

Below, I insert a previously written account as it is too painful to keep revisiting, and Justice has been denied time and time again.

There was not one single response or gesture of concern from any elected Representative, member of Congress or staff.

After requesting assistance from a number of lawyers in NY I realized that they were too deeply connected with the Democrat Party, and thereby compromised or deadly afraid of the NY Bar Association – what a way to perpetuate injustice! They held onto my material and testimony for weeks, well past statutes of limitations for ordinary crimes.

But these were violations of Civil and Human Rights, "Color of Law Abuses," Section 18, 242 and 243 of the Federal Code. *There is no Statute of Limitations, just a limit on the availability of an honest, courageous litigator.*

The three "winners" from the Manhattan DA's Office were out of a horror movie and two from the Brooklyn DA were also devious, but slicker, of a different caricature.

One of the Manhattan DAs was William Beesch, who dismissed all charges against persons harassing Republicans at the Convention held in NY. Beesch also sabotaged the prosecution of illegal alien, Carlos Guzman who had made the attempt on my son's life. Beesch tried to say that he was a "homosexual young man" *who couldn't possibly have tried to render my son unconscious before assaulting him with a machete. Beesch also tried that Carlos Guzman was defending himself from a homosexual advance from my very heterosexual son.*

When I asked Beesch to explain the concealed lethal weapons, Beesch became quite huffy and said he shouldn't be speaking to me. No he should have been doing his job and arresting and prosecuting Guzman,and investigating him for the untimely death of Jesse Sanabria and the battery of another teenager on Roosevelt Island, an assault for which another teenager was framed. All the youth on the Island knew it but were too terrified of Guzman and his baseball bat.

But he had "graduated" to tire irons and machetes when he came to my attention.

The clerks at the 114th Precinct refused to give me a Report Number for both attempts on my life.

The harassment continued day and night until I left. Stalking, watching, phone intercepting.and diverting. The intercom system was rewired to the telephone, allowing anyone to tap or intercept. There was no let up. We became REFUGEES FROM THE USA.

Same with my son, the object of the murderous hatred of the "silverback" since she first set eyes on the beautiful "white male" infant, carried in my arms to the apartment next door to the Lenox Hill Democrat Club's No 1 hate merchant, vote rigger and crime enforcer.

He was subjected to systematic demoralization at the Stalinist PS 217, to harassment, false arrest, physical abuse and more, by Roosevelt Island Public Safety and the racist, drug dealing thugs they protected on the Gulag. Many on Public Safety belong on the Sex Crimes Registry – some are already there – and must be investigated and prosecuted as DOMESTIC TERRORISTS if there is ever to be justice or safety on Gulag 10044.

VIII

FROM LAWLESS AMERICA, SUBJECT 984

August 16, 2012 A SUMMATION OF VIDEO TESTIMONY SCREENED FOR CONGRESS, JAN 2013

On August 16, 2006, I went for a walk between 3 and 4 pm. Seeing that the set for Brave One was struck, I abbreviated my walk and started my return home early. The presence of outside film-makers, one of whom was well acquainted with my family, controlled the abusive conduct of Public Safety (RIPS) and was the only reason I felt free to walk outside.

As I turned back onto Main Street a female RIPS thug, unknown to me, came up behind me and started to shout that I was 'having a stroke,' and told me to go and talk to the RIPS creature in front, again, a foul smelling person not of my acquaintance.

He started to say I was having a stroke and had to 'go with him.'

I said I wasn't and to call my daughter. He said he couldn't call on his radio, and I said radio the office and he said he couldn't and I started to walk away from him, across the zebra crossing btw RIOC offices and the nail salon.

The creep and convicted pedo-perv/sex offender (N.C. conviction) RIPS Toro was waiting on the other side and both he and Smelly came on either side telling me I could not go home.

I started to feel afraid and tried to get into the chapel, which was locked. Big mistake as it gave them a chance to block the path so I could not proceed. I was beginning to feel light head, and then sat down outside the chapel, realising that they weren't just playing stupid games, that my life was now at stake, and feeling shocked and faint.

The Maintenance Manager came by, saw RIPS became very concerned and said he'd call my daughter. I should have grabbed his arm and gone with him but creep Toro was between us.

When Woody was out of sight, Toro grabbed my arms and pulled them behind me, applying hand cuffs, sadistically tightening them, so they impeded circulation, and smirking, said, "you're not under arrest."

I responded that "I know that. I have committed no arrestable offense. Now take them off." Toro and Smelly then dragged me to 560 Main Street where EMS RUGER and FELLARIA were waiting. RUGER, a psycho, went into action, starting to shout into my face whenever anyone passed by:
"How much have you drunk! How many pills did you take! Why are you suicidal? How many pills! Are you having a stroke! You're having a stroke!"

I do not take medications, have a half glass of port at Christmas and Easter, and had no sign nor symptom of a stroke. This was a frame up. Anyone with half a brain knew I didn't use Big Pharma's products and seldom used alcohol, and then, very little, say at Christmas or Easter. However most of the Island were of the Woodstock Generation, with "drug fried brains" and were, thereby incapable of rational thought.

Fellaria remained silent.

Given the choice between remaining silent, considered 'crazy'/drunk/drugged and dead, or being 'crazy' and alive, I started to call out to the passers-by to "Contact the NYPD!" "Please call the NYPD!"

Psycho Ruger looked at Toro and said

"You didn't tell me she'd be like this."

They then pushed me off the kerb into the road hot sun, where I noticed an ambulance standing by. I became very afraid and started to remember rumours of RIPS seduction of black teenagers, o
f missing persons, of their assaults against my son, at least those of which I knew; of their many out of control crimes against me, of the 21st St. subway rapist, etc., burglaries by "uniformed police officers" all with the deceitful and sinister modus operandus of the RIPS thugs. Disappearances and untimely deaths!

A gentleman who knew me – no name, for his safety – miraculously passed by at that time and asked what he could do. And I said to please call my daughter and the police. He did, thus saving my life.

My daughter arrived. I asked her to call the NYPD and she did so. A sergeant and officer quickly arrived. They were confused at first but aware of the incompetence and abuse of RIPS. While they were talking to my daughter, TORO and SMELLY grabbed my person and dragged and lifted me into the lurking Ambulance.

This *was an illegal transfer as only EMS are allowed to bring persons into the 'buses' and 'restraints' on EDPs must be cloth and authorised by an MD.* I was neither an Emotionally Disturbed Person, nor ill. I had mentioned to two Soros minions that I was working on a book pulling together the threads of global terrorism about two weeks previously.

NYPD ordered RIPS to remove the cuffs. They didn't.

(NYPD 114th clerks later refused to give me a Report Number on this.)

NYPD called an EMS supervisor, an older woman, who was confused and over her head. She arrived and told me I *had* to go the ER. She was not very intelligent, nor did she seem aware of nor interested in the rules, just the *cover up.*

I told her I did not have to. I told would not go in that ambulance. That it was out of order, and used for criminal intent. I was becoming very weak, and my words were halting. I stood up inside the ambulance, but between the hypoxia, restricted circulation and extreme stress, my blood pressure was over 200 systole and approaching 200 diastole and the NYPD Officer, in a kindly and courteous tone recommended that I sit down again. It was not an "order." They were as bemused as I was and had seen enough of the overpaid goons, aka RIPS to be very concerned on my behalf, but it was, by some legal acrobatics, RIPS territory. NYPD with advanced training and experience, top of the line guys, forced to take directions from thugs and criminals with three weeks training!

In insisting that I go to the hospital in that ambulance, she became complicit in the crime of abduction, kidnapping with intent to rape and murder me, and the Color of Law Abuse.

1. Only a qualified EMT or Paramedic may transport a person into a NYC ambulance or "bus."
2. If restraints are used, they must be soft, not handcuffs.
3. Restraints may only be used on Emotionally Disturbed Persons.

4. Restraints may be only be used with the permission of a qualified doctor.

I was dragged into that ambulance by two felons, one of whom is a registered sex offender and who mauled me as he pushed me onto the cot. That was the freak Cesar aka Wilson Toro or Torres, later incarcerated in North Carolina for attempting to lure and molest children in McDonalds.

I was still in handcuffs, despite never having committed any crime.

It was strongly rumoured that New York's landlords paid EMTs to remove unwanted tenants, i.e., senior citizens living in rent controlled apartments. Ruger and Fellaria certainly seemed quite comfortable committing the felonies of abduction and kidnapping. In such a case they would also be in a position to rob said citizens of every valuable they could put their hands on.

NYPD PO Bouraisis (I believe that was his name. The Sgt had an Irish name, Kelly or Kennedy) persuaded me to go to obtain evidence that I was neither drinking, nor having a stroke nor drugged, and was fully compos mentis.

By that time I was very weak, in shock, and unable to sustain my contention that using that Abduction Ambulance would legitimise the felony in progress and that I would go in another 'Bus.'

After I was wheeled in to the Elmhurst ER, Ruger and Fellaria walked by my gurney, stopped and gave me the most spiteful and hate-filled look, analogous to that given by HRC against President Trump at the GHW Bush funeral.

Thank God, the doctor at Elmhurst was from Central America and well acquainted with political tyranny and abuse of taxpayer resources. He was kindly and professional, and did all tests necessary to prove the wannabe assassins WRONG!

ER doctor at Elmhurst confirmed my status and discharged me when my *now stress elevated* BP started to diminish. The systole was almost 200.

COMPLETE LOCKDOWN OF ALL AUTHORITIES; OF ALL INVESTIGATION; OF ALL VICTIMS SERVICES; HEADS DID ROLL AT RIOC, HOWEVER, BUT DID ME LITTLE GOOD.

NOV 2 2006

After months of stalking, harassment, intimidation, etc. RIPS tried again - this time to push their way into my apartment.

They called in the FDNY, the EMS, (Psycho Ruger again) looped my phone line and told my neighbours they were after a 'very dangerous person.'

My neighbours knew me as nurturing and kind and were disgusted. Exception being the instigator, one Roslyn Fernandez, mother of a drug addicted prostitute, grandmother of a convicted felon (attempted murder, multiple stab wounds) and local Co-ordinator for the Board of Elections, and Democrat THUG.

After intense, escalating warfare against me and a friend, I called the NYPD directly, and Sgt Tommassaro came out.

While I had immense respect for him, an army of thugs was behind him and would have pushed in my door if I opened it fully, and allowed him inside, so I kept the chain on and spoke through the cracks, explaining the situation to him. I showed him my "Thank You" letter from the late, great, Saint Mother Teresa of Calcutta.

He told them to get lost, and left.

They returned, and I called the 114th Precinct again. Tommassaro told them he would arrest them all if they didn't cease the harassment, and most departed.

The EMS, led by Capt. /Lt McLaughlin hung out on the ramp, McLaughlin calling, repeatedly trying to persuade me to 'just talk' to them - in order to gain access to my home.

I had enough of McLaughlin when my late husband was dying: he wouldn't give him Oxygen without taking him back to the hospital that destroyed him in a bumpy ambulance in the deep of winter; he camped out in my bedroom, monopolising my phone for *two hours,* so that our daughter, searching Manhattan for an O2 canister, could not call in and hear me tell her to get home stat, her dad was 'waiting for her' but would not be able to hold on.

He called the NYPD who came, but *respected poor Dermot's DNR and my Health Care Proxy and left.*

Eventually McLaughlin, Ruger and cohorts left, but it was evident that I could not remain on Roosevelt Island and I left the USA to house sit in Ireland, returning only to deal with the post Mitchell Lama Multiple Civil Rights violation contemporaneous and related to the extreme action of RIPS.

"They want your apartment, Deirdre..." Chief of Building Safety, NY

There's more.

Years of harassment, interference into my Right to Work, into my Freedoms, from Fear, Want and Religion, forcing me to become a REFUGEE FROM THE USA. This includes a Research project at Goldwater Hospital with NYU, theatre productions, literary opportunities and the opportunity to work in Intel in DC. The harassment extended to my son and caused serious disruptions in my family.

I have a body of work archived in the National Library of Ireland, and many honours and awards preceding my move to the Island of Doom.

The movie "Dark Water" was filmed there. The Good Shepherd Church was the production base. I would go upstairs to the chapel/community area and play spooky music on the organ. The crew seemed to like that.

Yet there was no redress for the crimes against me. No Victim Services. No investigation, utterly rude and uncouth by various Manhattan and Brooklyn ADAs. Pillars of society?

Each and every one that I encountered too vile to even sweep the streets.

IX

July 20, 2012

RECAP

I was a GOP Pro Life and International Relations Team Leader, and GOP campaigner on four Presidential Elections, the only Republican Conservative on Roosevelt Island to be so identified.

From the day I moved to Roosevelt Island, New York State employees have committed many "Colour of Law" offenses against me and my family. These appear to be instigated by a hostile Board of Elections co-ordinator with links to the municipal hospitals, RIOC HR, Housing and Public Safety. Her grand-daughter, a convicted felon, (attempted murder, multiple stab wounds, now a 'surgical assistant...' with an adjusted name) also assaulted my son with impunity.

These have been covered up at State and City level.

They include: assault and battery of my son; hounding, stalking and harassing of me and my son; aiding and abetting in the attempt on my son's life; obstruction of justice in felony attempted murder; probable obstruction of justice in attempted rape; dereliction of duty and racial prejudice in an assault on my son, etc., ad nauseum.

For me the most notable were the attempts against my life on August 16th, 2006 and Nov 2, 2006.

With regard to my son, the assaults amounted to a war, a war instigated by Board of Elections coordinator and Rangel protegée Rosalind/Roslyn Fernandez, a Board of Election Co-ordinator, Officer of the Lenox Hill Democrat Club, President of the "Ladies Auxiliary" at

Goldwater and Coler Hospital, i.e., "jobs for votes" program, along with her convicted felon granddaughter, an illegal Columbian assassin, apparently protected by her, and the 'army' of corrupt and perverted Roosevelt Island Public "Safety" thugs aka employed by New York State. "Gestapo" is too intelligent a word for them, although their conduct is comparable.

This war included multiple counts of assault and battery by "Safety" attempted sexual battery by 'safety' threats and intimidation by the thug-gang leader son of the RIOC Human Resources Director, false charges by Fernandez and her convicted felon grand-daughter and assault and battery by said grand-daughter.

While many senior executives of Roosevelt Island Operating Corp have been 'let go,' collateral to these felonies, their refusal and the refusal of the NYPD, DA, Mayor's Office, Attorney General (then Cuomo) to investigate, provide Victims' Services, respond to FOIL requests, and provide compensation for personal and professional losses is a gross violation of the Civil Liberties and Human Rights of me and my son.

I have provided detailed evidence of the 'Color of Law' offenses on video as part of a documentary which will be presented to Congress. Please advise if you would like further information regarding the politically motivated assaults of August 16th 06 and November 2, 06.

I did not know on August 16th that Jordan had struck the set and left, and so I was not prepared for the ambush that followed as I attempted to return to my apartment.

Details later, but it was a clear and unequivocal attempted abduction with intent to murder. Two rogue EMTs were also waiting – presumably with rohypnol or some other paralysand prior to rape and murder. One was very aggressive, wired. His name was Ruger. He showed up at the second attempt on Nov 2. His partner's name was Fellaria, and he was completely silent but complicit throughout.

By God's grace I survived that, but on Nov 2, 2006, a second attempt was made to take me from my apartment and finish the job.

About a month prior to the first abduction, I witnessed a tall, skinny man in a burqa sitting in a disused children's playground, staring across the river at Manhattan – or also in his sightlines was Rivercross, the HQ of Move On dot org and other Democrat freaks. Soros was also a regular visitor to the Gulag.

Naturally protective of children, I tried to get a "fix" on the burqa, but he would not look me in the eye. Only the eyes were exposed.

Suddenly a hand came out, the movement slow but menacing. It was a male hand, effete, light brown. It looked like the hand of a practiced killer.

To the outsider, ballet may seem like an "effete" activity, but it is combination of athleticism and art. The athleticism requires great physical endurance, personal discipline, and concentration, while the artistry involved offers many gifts, not least of which is reading body language, and expressing emotion both subtle, intense or violent, with the slightest movement.

I recognized that hand on a news program, showing Obama lifting a cup of tea from a tray. The menace was gone, the movement was casual, but it was the same hand.

There is no doubt in my mind that was Obama in the playground, and that the ubiquitous CCTV cameras allowed the criminals at RIPS to quickly identify me once he reported the incident.

He may have been there for a Move on dot org meeting for his impending campaign, or because a little girl the image of Sasha - and about the same age - lived on that island, with what appeared to be a nanny, and unlike other children, she never participated in any of the rare Island programs, just waiting for her new "Daddy" to pick her up – the man with the hand in the deconstructed playground.

The De-Construction of the United States of America was a long time in the planning.

Some names for Roosevelt Island:

    The Gulag

    The Roosevelt Island Gulag

    NY Gulag 10044

    Swamp Area 10044

    Isle of Woe

    Isle of Vile

    Isle of Loons

    Loony Toons Island

    Stalin's Revenge

    West Beijing

    Alinsky Island

    Helltown

    Hitlerville

    Naziville

Alien-nation

Pre "experiment" names: Hogs Island, Welfare Island, Blackwell Island.

Pre development use: Hospitals for the indigent. Prisons. Labor camps. Homes for female Irish immigrants suffering from nervous breakdowns. Lunatic asylums.

Early access: by rowboat. Later, elevator shaft down the side of the 59th Street Bridge support. This would have worked for the private residents on the developed Island, allowing pedestrian access to Manhattan when the various forms of transportation failed, but that did not fit with the Alinsky principles.

Final access: by "God help us!" "Alphabet" subway, i.e. no certainty as to which train returns to Roosevelt Island; broken down buses, dangerous walks, costly, risky taxi service. Private car, for those in taxpayer funded jobs such as the UN and / or NY City and State.

Destroying lives and entrapping victims – they couldn't wait to unfold this across the entire USA.

X

FRANKFURT AM HUDSON
<u>When Outcomes Fail, Just Change the Theory –</u>

Before WWI, Marxist theory held that if war broke out in Europe, the working classes would rise up against the bourgeoisie and create a communist revolution.
Well, as is the case with much of Marxist theory, things didn't go too well. When war broke out in 1914, instead of starting a revolution, the proletariat put on their uniforms and went off to war.

After the war ended, Marxist theorists were left to ask, "What went wrong?"
Two very prominent Marxists thinkers of the day were Antonio Gramsci and Georg Lukács. Each man, on his own, concluded that the working class of Europe had been blinded by the success of Western democracy and capitalism. They reasoned that until both had been destroyed, a communist revolution was not possible....

Ibid: In 1918, Lukács became minister of culture in Bolshevik Hungary. During this time, Lukács realized that if the family unit and sexual morals were eroded, society could be broken down.

Lukács implemented a policy he titled "cultural terrorism," which focused on these two objectives. A major part of the policy was to target children's minds through lectures that encouraged them to deride and reject Christian ethics.

In these lectures, graphic sexual matter was presented to children, and they were taught about loose sexual conduct.

Ibid: <u>The Birth of Cultural Marxism</u>
All was quiet on the Marxist front until 1923 when the cultural terrorist turned up for a "Marxist study week" in Frankfurt, Germany. There, Lukács met a young, wealthy Marxist named Felix Weil.
Until Lukács showed up, classical Marxist theory was based solely on the economic changes needed to overthrow class conflict. Weil was enthused by Lukács' cultural angle on Marxism.

Weil's interest led him to fund a new Marxist think tank—the Institute for Social Research. It would later come to be known as simply The Frankfurt School.

In 1930, the school changed course under new director Max Horkheimer. The team began mixing the ideas of Sigmund Freud with those of Marx, and cultural Marxism was born.
In classical Marxism, the workers of the world were oppressed by the ruling classes. The new theory was that everyone in society was psychologically oppressed by the institutions of Western culture. The school concluded that this new focus would need new vanguards to spur the change. The workers were not able to rise up on their own.

As fate would have it, the National Socialists came to power in Germany in 1933. It was a bad time and place to be a Jewish Marxist, as most of the school's faculty was. So, the school moved to New York City, the bastion of Western culture at the time.
In 1934, the school was reborn at Columbia University and its foreign born members began to exert their ideas on American culture.

It was at Columbia University that the school honed the tool it would use to destroy Western culture: the printed word.

The school published a lot of popular material. <u>The first of these was *Critical Theory.*</u>
Critical Theory is a play on semantics. <u>The theory was simple: criticize every pillar of Western culture—family, democracy, common law, freedom of speech, and others. The hope was that these pillars would crumble under the pressure.</u>

That was the theme of Freud's 1890 tome – "Civilization and its Discontents," a full frontal attack on Western Christian culture and civilization and an "intellectual" permission slip to decadence and depravity.

Next was a book Theodor Adorno co-authored, *The Authoritarian Personality.* It redefined traditional American views on gender roles and sexual mores as "prejudice." Adorno compared them to the traditions that led to the rise of fascism in Europe.

Is it just a coincidence that the "speed dial" slur for the politically correct today is "fascist" when the hell is always caused by the Communists!!!

And then they conceived one of the most lethal social experiments in the History of the World – Roosevelt Island, aka "The Gulag," or Helltown, or "Alinsky Island" or "The Gates of Hell."

"They" being the Rothschilds through the Columbia U "Institute for Social Research; the Rockefeller cousins – death in "flagrante delicto" Nelson "broke the ground" and the other cousin – FDR – was the inspiration for the

experiment. Eleanor Roosevelt was an early architect of "social engineering," prevailing on NY Governor Louis Lehrman to raze Irishtown to the ground, displace the residents and build Projects for the new black colony of economically dependent 'Rat voters, i.e. the new "Plantation!"

On the Gulag, the landscapers were a Rothschild partner, and ensured that not a single square inch of land was free from electronic and other surveillance. Except no tapes nor data were ever available when the Gestapo, aka "Roosevelt Island Public Safety" committed their heinous crimes against the residents, and, especially, our children.

I am sure that 5,000 rabid Democrats will dispute that and say what a wonderful place it was to raise children, to live, even as drugs disproportionately destroyed their childrens' lives; even as black youth harassed whites, and white kids were arrested for defending themselves against black harassment; even as the demographics kept changing, as access to and from the Gulag became a nightmare; even though the lower income residents, Dem'rat et al were brutally leveraged off the island once the "Mitchell Lama" program , i.e. *experiment*, was completed, and the mediocre rental apartments given a lick of paint, laminated (plastic) fake wood floors and silver fridges, and sold for hundreds of thousands of dollars.

The New York Times reported that only one family left after the experiment concluded, other estimates were closer to 600 families harassed, pressured, emotionally tortured into giving up their homes. Even Hitler would be envious at the secrecy and media collusion of the RIOC thugs.

Many had nervous breakdowns or turned to prescription psychotropic drugs as they were put into artificial debt by NY State, debts averaging $50,000 and de facto forcibly moved from their long term homes by complicit Housing Court Judges and officials, i.e., issued unjust eviction orders and dispersed around the tri State area – which also facilitated minimal inter communication, a tacit form of censorship.

On paper, the "tenants" voted to leave the Mitchell Lama Program. However, it was done thus. *RIHM, i.e., Management appointed 6 committee members who would vote on behalf of the 5,000 tenants!*

As egregious as that commie creep from Jamaica, a "Mr Bethune," who *completely voided the 4th Grade class election of my son Peter as Class President.*

One of the appointees was uncomfortable with the situation and made that clear; however, it was also made clear to her that voting with the "people" would have consequences, whereas voting with Management would be beneficial, and so her longed for co-op apartment in Rivercross suddenly became available.

Except, now she's stuck with them. Pity. I liked her.

By the time that vote came around, most of the residents on the Gulag were sufficiently tamed and subdued by Rat Party "kool aid," fluoridated water, the exhaustion of dealing with the daily exigencies of life on an Island patterned after Communist architecture and providing one of everything, i.e., no choice in grocery store, café, restaurant, and the most inefficient and exhausting method of transport on and off the place – well programmed to howl "we want/we love the tram." "We are the tram," "the tram makes us unique…" Even when the darned thing was *struck by lightning* after RIOC Pres blew off RIPS attempted abduction – murder and they were stranded for hours suspended by rope and using a blanketed off bucket as a make-shift bathroom, they clung to the tin box on the wheelie wire as their identity and status symbol. NO EXIT indeed.

They had been tested and found to be malleable, gullible "Useful Idiots." So instead of *tenants* voting whether to leave Mitchell Lama, *Management,* in collusion with the Dem'rat mafia run RIRA (Residents' Association) appointed five or six members of RIRA to "The Board.

Management, i.e., RIHM, staged a public meeting in the Good Shepherd Church cum Community Center cum Boardroom cum Theatre i.e. "one size fits all" space. Not a prayer centered place then.

Tables were set up and connected along the altar front. Seated at those tables were about a dozen people most of whom were neither identified nor identifiable. One did look remarkably similar to Loretta Lynch, former Brooklyn DA and Obama's Attorney General.

The head of RIHM, Doreen "two mercs" Isely, strutted about answering every question, whether directed to her or another party, *with the same answer to every question*, irrespective of its content. That answer was "People on Section 8 will receive "sticky vouchers" which they can take anywhere in the USA.

Seriously?

We're going to uproot you from your community, your friends, your parish, your support network, your apartment and make you homeless, but once you find a low rent apartment we'll send you a sticker????

As calm and polite as Dorene Isely appeared – and she was more civilized, or better groomed than the other apparatchiks – she ran a cruel and lethal operation to drive off the "lab rats" and commercialize the rat maze, i.e., Eastwood.

She *quadrupled the rents and then filed eviction notices when tenants were, inevitably, unable to pay and put into false debt – another stratagem now being used to displace citizens across Europe in order to allow politicians and Gardai (Irish Police) to buy up houses for peanuts then rent them to incoming "colonizers" for hefty rents paid by social services, i.e., the taxpayer. Same in Washington State, but at a different, more covert or surreptitious scale, and directed to the infiltration of jihadis. Those would be Saudis buying up apartment complexes, turning them over to HUD, then hiring ACORN trained managers to harass Seniors, Military, vulnerable residents, e.g., single parents, out of their homes and replace them with young Mid-Eastern men, fit and trained to fight, but with no English to facilitate integration.*

Two years after they succeeded in emptying one complex in Olympia, the jihadis went on a rampage, such as occurs in Europe. They burned and damaged up to 15 cars.

It also appeared that most of the Housing Court Judges were aware of the strategy and *in full collusion with the Gulag.* As long term residents after even longer term resident was served eviction notices for <u>artificially contrived, inflated and unlawful "arrears,"</u> all but one

Judge went along with it without question. They were ordered to give up their apartments or pay the huge, unjust debts.

These were created by RIHM arbitrarily and suddenly quadrupling rents.

There were two honest justices in Housing Court. One had retired by the time this debacle started and was replaced by Sabrina Kraus, the "pit bull" lawyer working for the vile and dishonest Iranian who turned sound older buildings into slums and unmercifully harassed tenants – Ari Kalimian. He supplied his Senior tenants with toy thermometers to assure them that their apartments were being heated according to the terms of NYC law, and it was Kalimian who destroyed our apartment and forced me to carry my baby in sub-zero conditions or with the oven on and open – extremely dangerous – and with ceiling bits and parts falling on my head.

It was Isely that advised the NY Times that "only one family had left." She had the deceptive attributes of the ACORN trained apparatchiks and was so slick and smooth a New York pimp could oil his hair with her lies.

Eastwood is now called "Roosevelt Island Landings." It hosts mostly middle to high income residents, and, up to Winter of 2018 at least, still has its share of perverts and corrupt "Public Safety" thugs.

Roosevelt Island Public "Safety" has grown exponentially at great cost to the taxpayer and disproportionately to the population and physical size of the island itself. It continues, unchecked, to engage in violence, assault, abuse, ridicule and harassment of tenants.

In January of 2018 tenants filed a complaint with the Inspector General for New York.

The saying "insanity is the idea that if you repeat something often enough the outcome will change."

Normally, I'd call that "optimism," depending on situation, weather conditions, prevailing, etc., but in the case of the unfortunate "remainers" on the biggest social experiment / hoax in the history of human kind, they still believe they are in a normal situation, where, if they keep repeating their lawsuits against individual Directors of Public Safety, Law and Order would miraculously float in and take up residence on Alinsky Island.

I agree with one aspect – it certainly requires a *miracle!!!*

XI

NIEMOLLER REDUX –

"And then they came for me…"

For a number of years, well before 2012, ambulettes plied up and down the one street bring patients from their long term homes in the Rehab and Residential Hospitals, and dispersing them around New York State, where it would be hardship for families to visit and find them.

No one on the Island gave a hoot. Aside from me and the chaplains.

And then they came for us…? Yes they did!

Oliver Chapin, the Protestant Chaplain, who lived on the Island after being forcibly removed with the rest of the Hospital staff from their perfectly fine "Nurses Residence," said to me that Roosevelt Island – the new, Main Street Utopian "Community," helped him to understand how Nazi Germany could do what it did to the disabled and then the Jews, under the very noses of decent but indifferent people. In order to facilitate "The Experiment," 600 perfectly fine apartments were allowed to disintegrate, Kalimian style, even as the housing shortage in NY became critical.

He was wrong about German "indifference," but that's for another time. Suffice it to say that it took 12 years, the murder of editors, disappearances of civilians, etc., to transform the mega state of Germany into the savage dictatorship controlled by only 7% of the population. *The*

Seven Percent Solution takes on a most sinister connotation given Freud and Hitler's Austrian connection!

On "Isle of Woe," not only were the liberal Democrats *indifferent, ab initio,* to the daily difficulties of Hospital residents, but many were *outraged* that their children would grow up with disabled people on gurneys and visible leg stumps wheeling themselves in and out of the stores, and so declared, openly. Some even moved away for just that reason. At least they were honest – unlike the 400 NIMBY Liberals that moved out every month once work began on the Section 8 building.

The people of Nazi occupied Germany initially spoke strongly against the disappearance of disabled patients and the hospital incinerators roaring night and day, and continued to try to speak until 12 years of disappearances, smashed presses, murdered journalists and editors finally subdued them into silent acquiescence with the horrors of Hitler's Germany.

There were no such restrictions or impediments on the Gulag, however. And yet all were silent. They "didn't know." *They did not want to know.*

There's a word for that. "NIMBY liberals." Not In My Back Yard. It translates thus: a Dem'rat politician shows up at a Press Conference to announce new funds for an initiative on behalf of the disabled, *id est,* i.e., s/he tells the public what a good fellow he/she is for using the public's money to move the disabled or provide a toy for them – anywhere but in his/her own "backyard!"

This was again dramatically manifest when a young homosexual, tall and gaunt, attached himself to my theatre company. The local liberals went howling for his blood. This was before AIDS had a name. The Christian Conservative protected him.

Again during a rehearsal, a talented older homosexual, a *professional* actor, was taunted by the NIMBY liberal actors on Loony Toons Island during an improvisation exercise. The conservative director, me, stopped it as soon as I realized what they were doing, but he left the show – and despite needing the professional credit, would not return. He died a year later, from the illness that had not yet been given a name. The others were amateurs, and as my late husband used to say "never work with amateurs." It is a completely different ethos.

Again, this has its roots in the Frankfurt School of Marxism and their "sponsors."

"The task of the Frankfurt School (ISR), then, was first, to undermine the Judeo-Christian legacy through an abolition of culture (Aufhebung der Kultir – Lukacs); and, second, to determine new cultural forms which would increase the alienation of the population, thus creating a "new barbarism."

In Roosevelt Island, they found the perfect place to do it. And succeeded beyond everyone's wildest imagination. The Rothschild landscapers took every inch of privacy; CCTV cameras everywhere except when needed by the public; private phone lines spliced into the intercoms and linked with Public "Safety;" lower income Americans envying better paid Europeans, working for the UN, East Europeans and Africans, multi-cultural divisions between Americans, most kids trapped by a toxic Public School system – scores maintained by the incoming Middle Class European and Asian children; multi culturalism is not cohesion. It is chaos, confusion, disunity. And so, on the toxic little Gulag, no one agreed with one another long enough to fight back. It was all, so, Politically Correct!

Political Correctness – Another Rothschild-Rockefeller Concoction

As always, there's more to the story here. Political correctness has roots in Marxism and Communism. Wikipedia notes that "In the early-to-mid 20th century, the phrase 'politically correct' was associated with the dogmatic application of Stalinist doctrine, debated between Communist Party members and Socialists." However, it goes back further to the Frankfurt School (Institute for Social Research) in Germany, which was set up in 1923.

The Frankfurt school was a think tank for social engineering, aiming to spread collectivism (or its offshoots of socialism, Marxism and communism) around the world. (http://www.unseen-pedia.com/political-correctness-rothschild-invention-language-control/

The Frankfurt School used WWII as an excuse for moving to its perfect home in Columbia U School of Sociology, i.e., "Socialism" where they could plan and develop the "perfect experiment" for the TAKEDOWN OF AMERICA, that is, Roosevelt Island, and its perfect rat maze, Eastwood, and the acquiescent multi-culti, Kool Aid drinking guinea pigs on Hogs Island.

Stalin's Revenge.

Rothschild's revenge for 1776?

It would appear that they are desperate to gain full control of their former Colonial "cash cow" and re-establish 100% autonomy over the 50 shining States of America.

"Nathan Rothschild had given Marx two checks for several thousand pounds to finance the cause of Socialism. The checks were put on display in the British Museum, after Lord Lionel Rothschild had willed his museum and library to them." Both of these key NOW families are thus implicated in Marxism, the Frankfurt School and political correctness..." humansarefree.com/2016/02/ political-correctness-rotschild.html"

Of course, the *taxpayer* is maintaining the treasures at great public expense in aforesaid Museum.

Just as the taxpayer is paying for the memorial to the FDR Roosevelts, ironically called the Four Freedoms, on the South end of the Gulag, across from the UN, and in the place where Pataki's appointee, Dr. Jerome Blue, had hoped to place a Marriott Hotel,

It's either naively ironic, or blatantly Alinsky-Lukasz and a tribute to the rest of the usual suspects, because the Gulag is an AFFRONT to the Constitutional USA where the Four Freedoms are violated on an almost daily basis.

Also ironic, because one of the Freedoms, is "Freedom from Want."

Had Dr. Blue achieved his goal of placing a Marriott at the south end of the island complete with water taxis to JFK – bliss! – training programs for youth; employment for youth and adults, "Freedom from Want" would no longer be an issue on that Isle of Loons. Otherwise, there was no employment on the Gulag. Waiters, store clerks, hospital staff, etc., all came from off Island! It was designed for despair and hopelessness. Those who praised it the most were Rat Party apparatchiks with second homes in Pennsylvania, NJ or upstate New York, mostly, it seemed, Pennsylvania! They probably vote twice; certainly Pennsylvania returned too many Democrats in the 2018 Midterms.

Then again, RIOC and the NYS / globalist goons running the Gulag got rid of the lower income residents by quadrupling their rents overnight and hounding them into Housing Court, nervous breakdowns and moving off that open air psych bin.

Yes, I know Merck suggests, i.e., the person who *refuses* the Kool Aid, e.g., the vegetarian in the Tribe of Cannibals is the crazy one. This in a chapter on mental health, yet.

Nasty aromas still emanating from that "stewpot!" And signs of "kuru kuru" in leading Democrats!

[1](See links re Roosevelt Island Public "Safety" at end of book.)

---

[1] See links re Roosevelt Island "Public Safety" at end of book.

XII

DIVIDE AND CONQUER - Swamp Area 10044

"Political correctness is a Rothschild invention. It comes from their think tank known as the Frankfurt school which was set up in 1923 to work out how to spread collectivism - or its offshoots, Socialism, Marxism and Communism - to the world. The real agenda of political correctness is to stifle objective investigation and free speech." Frankfurt School now operates out of Columbia U, Obama's "alumnus!"
https://toolsforfreedom.com/product-p/1495.htm

The "guinea pigs" / lab rats started moving into the gulag in 1974, but the experiment was planned long before.

I conjecture that it was a response to the defeat of Nazi Germany and Stalinist Russia, both of which were strongly influenced, if not supported and/or driven by the war broker Rothschilds. Stalin defected to FDR and FDR rewarded him by giving the Soviets control of faithful Poland, Hungary, Czechoslovakia and the other Eastern European countries. Other than that, yet another attempt at global domination had been thwarted by "the Americans," and something had to be done!

The Rothschild's are reputedly implicated in funding Napoleon, Hitler, Mao, Stalin, Lenin, Marx, Freud, among most despots in Europe. Their apparent M/O is to select a person with a similar language and culture to the citizens of the nation targeted for conquest. Example - Napoleon was a French Speaking Corsican set against France, Hitler - an Austrian dominating Germany, Stalin a

Georgian sicced on Russia; they managed to get the German Hanovers onto the English throne, East German Merkel on West Germany, and so on, all in the path to global domination.

The similarity of the chosen despots to the target population inspires trust, confidence – "one of us" acceptance.

On the other hand, the despot of the day is filled with a sense of exclusion, of not fully belonging, of inferiority, and deep resentment. S/he knows s/he is *not* "one of us," and the more s/he sees of the prosperity and privilege to which his/her hosts have always been accustomed, the more fiercely s/he hates them.

Their other strategy is "divide and conquer, suppress and starve." "Divide and Conquer" may explain why there are so many "North–South" divisions: North Ireland, South Ireland, North Korea, South Korea, North Vietnam, South Vietnam, Northern Nigeria, Southern Nigeria, East Germany, West Germany, and, of course, the Mason Dixon line in the USA, and the constantly provoked black vs white racial tensions.

Maps from the Yalta conference are significant, in that they show the sense of entitlement with which Rothschild's representatives FDR and Stalin were willing to carve up Germany, Europe and the entire world, with the reluctant consent and collaboration of Winston Churchill.

When the divided nations are eventually united, it is usually the Christians who concede, hence the spread of Communism and Islam in the late 20th and early 21st centuries.

"Suppress and starve." Currently an oil rich nation is in chaos, the people fleeing over the border to Columbia for basic food supplies. Venezuela is rich in fruits, vegetables, roots, arable land, fish, coffee, and the people, at least up to recent times, are intelligent and literate. While the ultimate NWO usurper, Obama was putting his feet on the White House desk or calling his terrorist cousin from the golf courses of America, the communists seized control of Venezuela.

Why destroy it?

Therein lies the rationale for the "boom-bust" economies. Allow the peon to work hard to achieve independence; then dump stocks or sell off currency, forcing the peon to close business or sell of the dream home – which the globalists then buy for a song.

There is a school of thought that believes that the Great Depression was caused by JP Morgan dumping stock because there were "too many yachts parked in my marina."

Same concept, only with an additional benefit to the "JP Morgans" in that they get to buy the entire marina and a few extra yachts as well, for rock bottom price.

This appears to be the system in Ireland at present, where homes are being seized at a rabid rate from mortgage holders as soon as they fall behind in their payments. If some are to be believed, it sometimes only a matter of days.

The homes will be refurbished, reassigned to a holding company then leased to the Government or Government crony for the benefit of incoming "migrants." Game, set and match to the Banks – most of which appear to Rothschild subsidiaries, in Ireland at least.

Destabilisation and chaos.

The Founding Fathers of the USA held them at bay, but they repeatedly found ways to sneak back in, notably with traitor Alexander Hamilton, fronting the Bank of New York for them, now devoured by Russia and absorbed into another NWO entity, the Mellon Banks. Their biggest coup, however is the Federal Reserve Act of 1913, signed under duress of blackmail, by Woodrow Wilson.

This gave them unprecedented power and control of the world's economy, and allowed them to set off a chain reaction leading to the Bolshevik Revolution.

After their other targets were depleted in every way, and the diabolical global domination strategy within palpable grasp, in come the 'Yanks' to plant defeat in the face of certain tyrannical victory.

Hold the tears! They always come out ahead in one way or the other. High profits from brokering war loans to every side in every conflict; Huge land and property grabs by scooping up devastated properties, from towns to estates to rural areas, all at rock bottom prices – even as the inevitable post war famines and epidemics take hold.

So in every war allegedly fomented by them, the *singular obstacle was American intervention, so America had to be taken down. The selection of the Kenyan/Indonesian/"who really knows" son of an American communist as the "Napoleon" to lead a stealth war against the USA is, then, almost inevitable. Like to the people, but not actually "of" the people. Hitler, the Austrian, sicced on Germany; Napoleon, the Corsican, sicced on France, Stalin, the Georgian, set upon Russia, Angela Merkel, the East German, set up to destroy West Germany, Obama, the Kenyan, tasked with taking down America, and in Ireland, an Indian-Irish LGBT moslem has succeeded in bringing in abortion to a nation already haemorrhaging populations to emigration. In other words, the name of the game is genocide. The gluttonous are aware that land mass does not increase, so they plan to minimise the population, while maximising their access to and ownership of every nano meter or foot of land on Planet Earth. Check out UN Agenda 21.*

In Castle Hospital, Hawaii, there is an alleged "MK Ultra Room" "in the basement" where a number of well-known public assassins were "treated." An eye witness who grew up in Hawaii and was about BO's age told me that BO had a Baskin Robbins kiosk at the base of that hospital – locational coincidence, perhaps, but he was also known as a drug dealer and male prostitute by his contemporaries, at least one of whom was "certain" that he was admitted to Castle Hospital.

Interesting. He certainly wasn't born there. "Reborn," perhaps.

Like Mark Chapman, like John Hinckley, both of whom allegedly had connections directly, or indirectly to Castle Hospital.

Methods used to persuade the American people to accept a person whom many politically savvy persons believe to be an imposter is analogous to the rise of Hitler.

Same methodology. Same brutal suppression of all dissenters. Same "disappearance" of the disabled;

The events in this account span a thirty year period, during which I and my children lived depleted, stressed, deprived lives, through no fault nor inclination of our own.

We were the victims of many horrendous crimes, as we were perceived as "white, Irish and unprotected." Every time I got something started or close to getting the hades out of there, "RF" the vicious neighbour, would somehow get wind and sabotage it. She was a semi-literate Democrat with enormous power through jobs for votes; an officer of the Lenox Hill Dem'rat Club, the local co-ordinator for the Board of Elections, etc., etc., with ears to the ground in every office where she ever placed an "ally," or, in other words, incompetent desperate to cling onto the job.

While I personally know of many Irish women driven out of their jobs and families driven out of their NY homes by blacks, and Democrat policies favouring blacks, I was fortunate to be raised in England where we learned to stand up to bullies, and where heroes, champions and reformers, both male and female, were held up as role models and examples. Yes, footballers were adored, but we didn't just reverence the physical; we were taught to respect character and heroism. Edith Cavell, Grace Darling, Elizabeth Fry, St Margaret Clitherow, and Florence Nightingale were some of our heroines; Churchill, Douglas Bader, St Thomas More, John Fisher, and the "greatest generation" were our heroes, especially our flying aces, the RAF, who lost up to 14 pilots per week but kept those amazing Spitfires dodging and swirling in the air, like swallows. And then came the Beatles, the Stones and drugs poured in from the Middle East the frontline in an undeclared war on the Euro Christian world and its values. The Irish were taught to "offer it up." The Americans just closed their parish halls, their homes, their taxpayer funded open spaces and the Dem'rats got what they wanted – a depleted, demoralised, frantic population, and the chance to regulate, regulate, regulate America's Free Spirit out of existence.

Everything that occurred here is true, most incidents are verifiable. Some, like the fundamental reports of the "Experiment," would require the expertise of Julian

Assange to discover and reconstruct, but I am an eye witness to the book length questionnaire issued by Columbia U School of Sociology and home of the Frankfurt School of Marxism, a bastion of treason, and to the closing of the experiment three decades later.

Moslems burning documents and newspapers in the barbecue pits at the secluded north end of the island after 9/11 are probably not verifiable, for example, despite an eye witness. I called 911. The operator, who would make Alexandria Ocasio Cortez seem intelligent, insisted it was a job for the "Fire Department."

I said "No, this is a job for the police." JTTF was formed shortly thereafter. I was shocked at their total naiveté with regard to global terrorism. Yes, they were good men, mostly, as far as I could see, and good "diggers," but *clueless,* utterly clueless.

Some names have been changed to protect the innocent – me, from abuse and litigation by the guilty – them.

My intent in writing this is to show that for thirty years the Constitution of the United States was under direct attack.

The intent by the Frankfurt School of Marxism – Columbia School of Sociopathy, erratum, Sociology, was to study methods of destroying Constitutional America on behalf of a Europe based syndicate / cartel /mafia / bunch of bespoke tailored gangsters.

XIII

THE MAGINOT LINE – Instant classism…

The Island was intersected by Main Street, which I quickly renamed "The Maginot Line."[i] Main Street went North South, dividing the original residential areas into Eastwood and three buildings on the westside – with a view of Manhattan's concrete buildings and the FDR Drive. Eastwood had the Ravenswood Power Plant. I called it my L.S. Lowry "Industrial Landscape." Despite the fact that rents in Eastwood were comparable to those on the West Side of the Island, there was a marked difference in attitude and attire according to which side of the street you "belonged." Eastwood dressed down. Westview, Island House and Rivercross dressed up in a "Rei – Birkenstock" sort of way. Drab but expensive, champagne socialist style. Exception in Eastwood being the East Europeans, the Russians conspicuously elegant in a clichéd "Natasha the spy" sort of way – short hair, collars turned up, tight pants, thigh length fur jacket or short leather jacks and high, spike heeled boots, almost a self-parody; the Romanians somewhat more "frumpy," while the Poles were more discreet in appearance.

The Maginot line defined our social status, in the "egalitarian" "utopia" aka Roosevelt Island.

The "lab rats" were in Eastwood, and there must indeed have been many sniggers among the "globalists in the penthouse suite" about the design of the massive, Soviet style building called Eastwood. It was, indeed, designed as a rat maze. Enter one door at one end, and come out two city blocks later at the other end, with a number of exits in between on multiple storeys. This eventually allowed me to evade the harassing Public Safety Gestapo, but made raising teenagers far harder than necessary.

The prize winning architecture was by Philip Johnson. It was a fire hazard, requiring torqued steps up or down to a tiny hallway - added to the physical stresses of life on the Gulag, blocked the Eastern sun and cast a shadow along the entire length of Main Street. No escape, No Exit!

This was later considered a factor in the high rate of recidivism, substance abuse, suicide, runaways and depression among the younger Island residents.

None of this was reported. Any statistics relating exclusively to Roosevelt Island are buried within Manhattan or Queens Meta data.

Aside from the now vanished records of the Columbia U / FSM experiments...

Later for that.

I was alerted to the globalist nature of Alinsky Island by the fact that while few Americans outside the NY RAT Party had heard of it, every multi culti "globalist" "in town" planted his or herself there - on the other side of the built in "Maginot Line," i.e., across Main Street from the Rat Maze.

There the left-wing professionals from every other country in the world lorded it over the blue collar Americans. Mr. "I hate America," i.e. George Soros, and the globalist bankers for whom he fronted never forgave the Founding Fathers for 1776 and the shot across the bow of tyranny that was heard around the world and which continued to fire throughout the French Revolution, the Napoleonic Wars and WWI, WWII. This made the "Empire" i.e., the desired globalist monolith harder to achieve and control. They would destroy the USA from within.

The Westview, Island House and Rivercross Apartments were "normal," functional architecture – Rivercross being considerably more luxurious than Westview and Island House. Most of the non-citizen foreigners and UN workers resided there, illegally benefiting from Mitchell Lama 226 subsidies.

The UN flooded to the Gulag; Koffee Annan was seen scowling at the bus stop every morning before his appointment to the Directorate. His Secretary, a white, Anglo Irish man named Erskine B Childers, son of executed Freedom Fighter Erskine A Childers lived there with his wealthy Thai wife and their son. Erskine told me that all the problems in the world were caused by the white Christian male.

He wasn't "white" when I'd finished with him, closer in color to beetroot!

Six months later, I saw him in the Gulag Post Office mailing his manuscript – "on the beneficial influence of Christianity on the world..."

He died soon after, a young man, in his fifties, if that. I never discovered if that particular manuscript was ever published. He seemed a sincere, if somewhat naïve man, but he could have just wanted to avoid another of my "lethal to liberals" lecture specials...

Many others lived on the Gulag - French Consuls, Italian Bankers and at least two Italian anti-Terrorist agents, German Bankers, ex CIA agents, authentic and self-styled, African UN Employees, English UN Employees, Egyptians, Moroccan diplomats and relatives of the King; Palestinians opened a deli there, a really incompetent Saudi agent showed up and bagged a job working for the Catholic Parish as secretary to the notorious Fr Miqueli. Robert Calvi, "God's Banker" hid out on the Gulag, after questions re the Vatican Bank's finances, before being hanged from a bridge in London, UK. The wives of the Mid East delegation belonged to "bruise of the month club."

The Secret Service accompanied the King of Tonga to Mass there while he was visiting friends – yes, Tonga knew about Insane Island, but Americans have never heard of it!!!

I was delighted to play the most patriotic hymns for the benefit of the Secret Service agents accompanying him. They were classy men and women then. I was not asked to play in Church after that until one Christmas when the now notorious Fr Miqueli said he "couldn't get anyone else" and was "desperate." How could I refuse an invite like that! Three Masses, didn't request a fee for any of them. A privilege to *play for the Christ Child...*

Bizarrely, the *American* taxpayer was double subsidizing the UN!!! They were *all* receiving Section 226 Housing subsidies in addition to their UN Housing subsidies. So many benefits, yet *they never stopped complaining!* They were afflicted with an extraordinary sense of extreme entitlement.

Those housed in the "Americans only" luxury Co-ops were also receiving mortgage subsidies – again, diehard

Democrats donors. I just wish I had taken notes as they bragged about their connections and associations with the left and far left, and amount of subsidy received relevant to their mortgages!

And of course, the infamous George Soros would show up from time to time, notably on Saturday mornings in election years, always with the same "cold, dead eyes" and group of Move on.org supporters. He looked like a nondescript owl, but without the intelligence, awareness and charm of the Strigidae, and certainly not the beauty!

While the Maginot demarcation was more social than economic, with professionals such as lawyers and accountants living in Eastwood, it was just one of many strategies in the demoralization of America's youth.

The "prestigious" West Side was home to well-paid UN apparatchiks with arrogant airs and spoiled children going to the UN school in limousines. They were from Europe, Asia, Africa, enjoying double Housing subsidies, ie, UN subsidies as well as Section 226. They were conspicuous consumers, well dressed, well nourished by luxury foods at the UN Commissary, sold at wholesale prices. More subsidies.

American children took the packed morning commuter tram or a private school bus with suspension never intended for the 59th Street Bridge. For many parents, the monthly fee was a hardship. For others, a song.

On "visual," say, by the "visitor from Mars," the Americans on the Gulag were poorly dressed "lumpen proleteriats," the least socially desirable, whereas the foreigners, non-Americans, were privileged, went on vacations abroad – subsidized again by the taxpayer every two years – or on ski trips. They were usually from two parent families, and the children of Europeans well mannered, well spoken.

There were occasional reports of African diplomats forcing their son to sleep in the basement storage units of the Island; and some of the Mid Eastern wives were members of the "bruise of the month" club.

The long term effect, however, was the subliminal inculcation of a sense of inferiority in the less privilege, less socially striated young Americans.

While black, brown and Asian kids were mostly left alone, Public "Safety" made a point of targeting the white kids of the Island.

Further demoralization– virtual castration, of America's future "white males."

In addition to the class warfare intrinsic to Philip Johson's "award winning" fire hazard housing plan, there is the interesting matter of the small businesses on the Island.

'One of each," i.e., no competition allowed. Businesses carefully selected. Very difficult to obtain leases.

RIOC would rather lose revenue than allow a non Dem'rat supporter to profit from the Island.

Initially, *one* small business was owned by Americans, Don and Lorraine, who established the first pizzeria and called it "La Piccola Mela." The food, incidentally, was excellent.

Big mistake, however. "Piccola Mela" translates as "Little Apple," and a t-shirt maker claimed the copyright on that title. He later went to work for an authentic plagiarist, one Stephen Spielberg who stole "E.T." from an author of childrens' books, - case settled out of court, but Spielberg continued to pick the brains of Truffaut and Attenborough, two great directors conveniently "cast" in Spielberg's early movies.

Bigelow Pharmacy was also American, a lovely addition to the Island in the early days until it was forced to move into Sloans, pay rent to rent-free Hillary donor, John Catsimatides and downgrade to just another storefront Pharmacy with the same, dull, schlock products as every other storefront Pharmacy in Manhattan.

The owner of the liquor store was a black Democrat called Archie Seale. His son went over to the "Rainbow Coalition" and was a decent guy. One day we learned that Archie Snr was the "Mayor" of the Island. No ballot, no election, no notification, just a clear hint that Democracy was NOT in effect on the Isle of Loons.

Aside from True Value, none of the other stores were owned by Americans, and True Value didn't last that long. People on the Island were desperate to be connected with the "outside" world that some were working without salaries. It was bizarre.

The rats were restless. The maze was becoming harder to navigate and incredibly boring.

The patron of the Deli was Greek. Allegedly he died of AIDS. The Green Kitchen was also owned by Greeks, and of course, Catsimatides was a Greek. When the Green Kitchen became the Trellis, two Greek cocaine dealers took over.

When I left the Island years later, the Deli was Palestinian who openly physically abused their employees. The flower shop was Romanian. Partly because it paid high rent and had few customers, it was believed to be a money laundering enterprise.

Two beauty salons were Korean and there was a Chinese take-away. The bakery owned by very nice Mexicans was closed by the Health authorities, despite being the cleanest eatery on the Island. No roaches, like the Trellis, no mice like the Chinese, but far worse – the Mexican owners turned out to be pro Life and … REPUBLICAN!!!

A couple of restauranteurs came and went quickly, and a bar, allegedly part owned by the publishers of the WIRE, opened up. A bar is almost essential for snooping in a society.

The overall effect was to inculcate the Gulag's *American* youth with a sense of futility and failure.

Foreign business were stable and thrived. Businesses owned by white Americans failed.

"Don't even try, kids!"

When Dr Blue was Pataki's appointed Director of RIOC, he opened some store-fronts to black operated businesses.

While Dr Blue meant well and was not, as far as I know, part of the "pack," his empowerment programs for the black youth again reinforced the message of the Island – "White is worthless."

Another subliminal for the children of the Island – America is hopelessness, despair, defeat. Non America is cool, hip, successful!

Columbia U, Rothschild, Roosevelt, Rockefeller. They thought of everything.

And then came 9/11. The Palestinian owned Deli was closed that morning.

Against the wishes of the nun, "we the people," opened the chapel for prayer all day every day for the duration of that week. Every page of scripture opened at random, was relevant to the horrors of Ground Zero.

And we learned, anecdotally, that most of the co-adherents of Mohammed Atta, etc., knew well in advance to stay clear of the Twin Towers on the eleventh of September, 2001.

From the deli owners, to the coffee carts, to the UN, to individuals in other professions – they *all knew.*

Except the new Director of the FBI – Robert Mueller and the person who appointed him, President George W Bush.

XIV

WELCOME TO AMERICA

I was born in a tropical island to a *soi disant* aristocratic Anglo German family and an Irish Nationalist father. Doomed from the start! Tired of internalising the conflict, I discovered Italy, the one place where I could be just a human person.

Unfortunately, due to the swamp creatures on the Gulag, America did not keep her promise of Liberty, Equality, etc.

Then again, the Gulag was not America as the world understands America. The Gulag was the anti-America, the sword in the back of Lady Liberty, the termites in the foundation of the Great Republic, the Judas, the natural home of Benedict Arnold and traitor banker, Alexander Hamilton.

It is no accident that he was the one Founding Father represented on Broadway during the "regime" of a treasonous imposter who has yet to be fully exposed.

***

My grandfather was an explorer, cartographer, broadcaster, with goldmines and coffee plantations. He had five living daughters and two sons. One daughter, Joan, died of cholera age nine. Her name was Joan and she was the second child. Not much was said about another deceased child.

My grandmother was blonde, blue eyed, the granddaughter of an Irish sea captain and daughter of a Jewish lawyer. The lawyer, Victor Abrams, had a business with a Royal Charter. He was the embroiderer royal to Queen Victoria. He eloped with my great grandmother, Emily Boyle of County Cork when she was 16. Her seafaring, widowed, father did not approve – possibly because Victor was English. Or he foresaw a life of landlubber loneliness.

Given a remarkable resemblance between members of my family and the descendants of QV I have often wondered if his prestigious appointment to the colonies had salacious over tones. There is reason to believe that he may have had a second family there too.

Aside from all that he played the violin and gave concerts for charity.

 Liberals allow Females to be beautiful or brilliant, not both. Feminazis are the most vicious on this score. Their goal was never about "elevating" femininity, but to destroy the energizing male-female dynamic, destroy the family and create a divided America, with "Communist style" families – both parents working, thus keeping the labour supply high and the wages low, and allowing the State and criminals to assume control of the children.

We now have breakfast in school, after school programs, day care centres for infants, etc., all depicted as a "good thing" irrespective of cause or consequence: broken homes, troubled kids, illiterate kids, latchkey kids, drop out kids, over stressed mom…drinks, drugs, the works, i.e. the transformation of supportive, highly functioning interstitial communities into destructive dystopias.

Back to the tropical island – very beautiful, and although I was only 10 months of age when I left it, I have strong residual memories, of vivid colours, of brightness, of perfumed breezes, hummingbirds, bougainvillea, hibiscus, of lizards, of my father killing a snake, of sitting on Grandfather Kellan's lap, "reading" the newspaper with him.

That love and sunshine was soon to disappear as my father's term as a Scientist for British Food Research ended, and he had to return to the foggy British Isles with his new family.

I arrived in England at 10 months of age, conversant in French and English after a three week journey on board the SS France.

Later, in Surrey, at two years of age, I read the account of the death of George VI in the London Times, and remember my parents joking about me "pretending" to read the paper. My father was seated, reading it, I was looking over his shoulder.

While I read the words I did not understand the context until the walk home from Mass, when my parents discussed it and I had an "oh that's what that's about" aka "Eureka" moment.

Notable memories include being brought to see the new Queen by our mother and to hear my father's left wing Irish Nationalist speeches at Hyde Park in London!

Nearly dying from Septic tonsils age 3, convent school age four, skipping kindergarten and a grade or two, at age six realising that other children did not read Shaw, Collidi, Wilde, etc., remembering the deep loneliness of realising I did not know how to play with them and that they did not understand a word that I said. I might as well have been speaking a foreign language.

Believing that Esso would move him to Ireland, my father took a job at the Fawley Refinery, and we moved to Hythe, Hampshire where two teachers, Mr. Mott and Mrs/Miss Simmonds nurtured and encouraged my gifts without making me feel like a freak show.

They gave me IQ tests and puzzles, challenges to do at home, allowed me freedom to write what I wanted, not holding me to assigned essays; they appointed me class librarian, and when I failed terribly at that, preferring to read instead of checking out books, they gave me two assistants. In the Foreign Office they call it "being kicked upstairs."

When tests showed that I had the "literacy equivalent of an Oxbridge graduate," at the age of nine, that was mentioned quietly, to me, not trumpeted all over the school nor broadcast in local or national media.

The sad, lonely, envied, unexplored world of the *female* child prodigy was briefly suspended.

And then we went to Ireland, where I won many awards, was splashed all over the National Newspapers, made my first appearance on RTE age 12, received a disastrous flu shot age 15, and spent most of fall, winter, spring in a sick bed recovering from one variation of pulmonary disease to another, and using willpower to stand upright and walk unaided.

Until I found a Homeopath and life began again. Offers started pouring in – a starring contract from Sergio Leone, a full Science Scholarship from British Rubber Research – not through my father; on my own merits, won some acting awards, was nominated "one of Ireland's outstanding young poets, etc., etc.

I refused to sign up to Sinn Fein / IRA. I objected to my father taking my little brothers to the crazy streets of Dublin to sell "An Phoblacht," a proscribed publication. This created many problems for my left wing father who oscillated between wanting a Russian peasant daughter and "Ireland's first female engineer/President." Serious, harsh tensions. Passport confiscated, etc., etc. I was 20!

Then I received a call from a neighbour whose nephew was in British Intelligence. "Get out now," she said.

I will always be grateful to the late Sheila Hardiman Scott for that call. She was a petite woman of great courage – drove heavy armoured vehicles onto transport ships during the war – *without* power steering. A heroic nature! She would have to live with my father's aggression after I left and she knew it and was prepared for it.

And from Ireland I went precipitously to NY to avoid recruitment into a family related extreme political organisation.

With one suitcase. A *de facto* refugee, *de jure* "emigrant."

From the frying pan into the fire.

How was I to know that NY was full of IRA supporters and fundraisers, and that my educated English speech was, to the descendants of the Irish Famine, like a lit match in a box of "gelignite"

Manhattan was totally different from anything I experienced in Europe. Some might call it exciting. It was certainly colourful if immensely lawless. Rapes, muggings, black panthers signing on the street, pimps and pimpmobiles driving from Harlem to hang out in Times Square…stoned out of their mind taxi drivers trying to run you down as you crossed the street on a green light; "Moonies" handing out roses, recruiting, recruiting; other cults sprouting like mushrooms across a dying America; women on stoops watching their children, while drinking coffee from coffee shops a block or so farther than their own kitchens. I had never seen a homeless person the street, outside the tropics; and I had never met an illiterate 12 year old until I came to NY.

It was never a good fit for a country girl homesick for the New Forest of England and the beaches of Bournemouth, Brighton and Ireland. I cried every day for the first two years.

Noise, noise, noise!

Angry, aggressive people, lured to the "greatest city in the world" expecting glamor and appreciation for work well done and finding plagiarists, thieves, closet sized apartments, muggers, streets smelling of urine, and the stone faced sadness of stubborn disappointment.

May late husband, Dermot lived in an older building on 425 East 80th Street, furnished with props from plays. The building was old, but sturdy, and everything worked – until Ari Kalimian landed in NY from Iran, bought it from the Rabbi's widow, the previous owner, and destroyed it around us.

Somehow, an Iranian refugee was able to arrive in NY, quickly purchase a classic building in New York City and then destroy the lives of many Americans while so many in that heartbreak city, worked their hearts out and ended up as Senior Citizens with nothing, or in four, five flight walk-ups, afraid and unable to move because the rents had soared.

Most of the people in 425 Eat 80th Street were American, many of Irish extract. It was the first time that I ever met a twelve year old girl who could not read. They were kindly people, "sit on the stoop" people, sipping from store bought coffee containers, watching or talking. St. Rita's Parish. St. Rita, with St. Jude, patron saint of the hopeless.

Every Friday in winter and summer Kalimian turned off the heat and hot water until Monday morning. It was turned on during the week because the City Housing

Inspectors were off duty....but switched off at 4pm Friday and back up on Monday morning when the corrupted inspectors would show up, find the heat turned back on, ignore the ongoing deterioration of the building.

Before this freak Ari Kalimian's man-made hell started, I had established the world's first theatrical celebration of Bloomsday, which provided employment to actors, and which was eventually stolen by Columbia U Professor of Drama, Isaiah Sheffer. His wife was on the NY City Council and thereby used her influence to obtain the Symphony Space Theatre for him at a "peppercorn" rent of $1.00 per year. He was an academic with no experience of producing in professional theatre.

That's where I, rather my late husband, brought my "Evening with James Joyce and Friends," and discussed our first "Bloomsday" in 1972, inaugurating "Irish Pub Theatre" at the White Horse Inn. I was not invited to that either, nor was my name put on the program as the writer-adapter. You can take the Irishman out of Ireland but you can't take misogynist Ireland out of the Irish man, especially when under the influence of, the drunken Scotswoman, Helena Carroll, who appeared in my works on Joyce and who then persuaded John Huston to make Joyce's "The Dead." I had worked with Houston in Ireland. Helena made sure I did not come to the performances. Poor Dermot, abandoned to Irish cousins age 2, then to monks, age 8, could never stand up for himself or his loved ones, God love him.

Ah the indissoluble bonds of whiskey!

Isaiah wanted to do one of my plays, for a "Weinstein." No way, schmuck!

Helena moved to California and became Ho'wood's "authority" on all things Joycean. No underestimating the fury of a woman scorned, the jealousy of women – Helena also knew that I had worked with Huston on "Sinful Davey" – and used it as her intro. Without me, "The Dead" might never have been made.

I was the first female performer to interpret James Joyce on the stage of the Symphony Space Theatre and have been written out of its history since.

With the collusion of kiss up Irish Consuls, who fawned over Sheffer, unwilling to believe that an unknown "wemmin" could do anything original.

Instead of being my ticket to a gentler home, the "Evening with James Joyce and Friends" and other dramas I constructed and co-produced, *bringing, initially, paid employment* to NY actors, was a gold mine and stepping stone for an unscrupulous and ambitious New York academe, a pompous Irish wannabe Senator, and the dying light of an angry, drunken actress.

Both Finola Flanagan and the McCourt brothers (Frank and Malachy) also "spun" their shows from mine, copying my format after Malachy joined us at his "Two Saints" village pub. Frank also plagiarised the "parrot" sketch from Monty Python.

Helena Carroll found her way from "Bloomsday!" to California, where networking with the Irish and Irish American theatre community, i.e. Lansbury, Flanagan, Angelica Houston, to Houston's production of the dead.

Ironically, when Elizabeth Taylor tried to revive her ex-husband's career by putting a ton of money into a Broadway production of "Blithe Spirit," a casting agent wanted to replace Helena with me, but Helena's agent, knowing her abrasive character, had a $35,000 buyout, so

I ended up coaching Helena in French – la bonne francaise – and she continued in the show.

Just as well – the night time commute from Helltown and back six days a week would have been both dangerous and devastating to my health which was beginning to seriously implode.

New York City turns you into hard steel – or coal dust!

And people wonder why President Trump sometimes seems abrasive!

You have a chance to transcend with decent accommodations, privacy, and the ability to walk to the store or subway without being pounced on by one of the 5,000 liberals with serious personal problems, but Alinsky Island just ground one down. An uninterrupted night's sleep was the only realistic hope or aspiration.

I'm no fan of the "descendants" of Freud, but if they belong anywhere, it's on the NY Gulag where Old Glory never flew and the Constitution of the USA was replaced by a Corporate Diktat and a small army of thugs.

XV

Isle of Woe - Swamp Area 10044 and Bezhmenov's List

Instead of a home with trees and grass, we got an apartment overlooking a power station on one side, but still, trees and a square of grass on the other side. After spending far too many years on Roosevelt Island, aka Swamp Area 10044, Alinsky Island, Loony Toons Island, etc., and experiencing far too many traps and interferences in my attempts to leave the crazy place, I came to realise that "The Paradise Island in the East River," the gun free, car free, electric bus free, crime free multiculti "Utopia" was a farce, a trap, a lie, an illusion.

The Queens diesel buses serving the hospitals traversed the island at least every hour. The free electric buses started to charge – in between breaking down every other day. The subway opening was delayed because the subway tunnel was too small.

So, for another couple of billion dollars, the corrupt mavens of New York City and State lined their pockets and the pockets of their friends again.

Meanwhile the island's youth walked back and forth to Manhattan in the N and R tunnels. These were highly risky, but preferable to paying the 'Island tax,' i.e. the subway fare, which originally didn't seem too horrendous, but by the end, as children quickly grew to full fare height, became prohibitive.

Staten Islanders, who lived farther from Manhattan had a free ferry to bring them back and forth.

Originally baffled by the sheer incompetence of the design and the constant hassles and harassments of daily life there, I came to realise that was *intentional.* There was no privacy. Nelson Rockefeller "turned the turf" at the inception of the Island; the landscaping was by a Rothschild partner, the overall architectural concept by globalist Philip Johnson – all designed to offer minimal, actual negligible privacy, except where the employees of New York State were engaged in the commission of crimes, then suddenly there would a complete dearth or absence of evidence.

I have sought online for evidence of Columbia U's involvement in this treasonous and spurious experiment but to no avail. Columbia U's School of Sociology was present at the beginning of the experiment and at the conclusion. Columbia U accepted a "Foreign Student" named Barack Obama, but there is no public evidence that he was ever required him to attend class or graduation. [iii]

I know for a fact, that a huge book of questions devised by Columbia U was distributed to each and every tenant in the early days. I found the questions alarmingly intrusive and returned the book, unanswered. This may have marked me out as a "trouble maker," a "thinker," a "dissenter."

This and a recommendation by Ambassador Curley, Ford's Ambassador to Ireland and Reagan's Ambassador to France, may have identified me as an Independent, or, "worse," a member of the Centre Right. I was certainly pro Life and vehemently anti Roe v Wade even though I felt extremely powerless in the face of the organised harpies and crones pushing for the murder of sweet and innocent pre-natal babies. In this they were aided and abetted by a slew of Hollywood movies, showing babies as an impediment to personal growth and children as intrinsically evil – "Rosemary's Baby," "The Omen," "The Children of the Corn," etc. There was little interest in countering the tsunami of child phobic agit-prop pouring in from Ho'wood.

I did, however, succeed in keeping the abortionists off the Gulag, by warning that it would also bring pro-Lifers to the Island! Dear, dear, the shock, fear and consternation in the eyes of baby butchers anticipating the arrival of little old ladies carrying rosaries was almost comical!

Little did I know or understand the incestuous nature of the Left wing, Democrat, covert Communist "tribes" running New York, Chicago, Los Angeles, Olympia, San Francisco, and a great deal of DC.

Around 2004, as the experiment was concluding, the pastor, Fr Gorman, RIP, asked me to speak with a researcher, one of many "wrapping up" the findings. I suppose I was the "control group," the lone dissenter, the pro Life Conservative, the "vegetarian in the Tribe of Cannibals." I learned nothing from the vapid grad student, but gave them the unpleasant truth about that Alinsky dump, that treasonous experiment in deposing the Constitution and imposing dictatorship upon residents, to be extended, if successful, across the entire USA.

As it was. Under Obama.

Soros was frequently on that Island, so much so that I suspected he had a co-op in the private blue wing in Rivercross, the subsidised luxury building for DemRat Commicrat apparatchiks. Move on dot org had two of the creepiest men organising it. They must have been very evil men because God doesn't do "ugly," and they were two of the ugliest men I have ever seen, in all ways. One dressed and bearded like a wannabe body double for Lenin, the other, Heaven help us, married the only woman *less well featured than her flat footed berk husband – it was not clear whether the attraction was ideology or money, but together they looked like twin subjects of a DNA experiment gone terribly wrong.*

Chicago's leading feminist found her way there, and picked my brains – more fool I – at every opportunity re drama construction, character work, etc. Another Liberal free loader and cheat. Although she was married, she actively promoted abortion, lesbianism, etc. But yes, in business or banks, she always preferred to deal with a man!

They were underhand, devious and malicious. A rum lot, indeed!

Was there ever a place so pretty and yet as desolate as the Island in the East Channel of the East River of New York, referred to here as "Alinsky Island" or "The NY Gulag." Riker's Island, a prison, the refuse dump for NY's far left social policies, takes the prize for desolation, with as much "beauty" as Dachau or any other Concentration camp. Harts Island, aka Potter's Field comes a close second, the difference being that the bodies interned at Harts Island are beyond the reach of the NY Communist apparatchiks.

Or are they? A freighter ran aground earlier in 2018. It was Chinese, but transporting the bodies of hundreds of Americans, chopped up for sale to Europe's Universities and, as yet unknown markets.

But New Yorkers, beleaguered with the agonies of the transport system, the discomfort of matchbook apartments, the ubiquity of cockroaches, the contiguity of beautiful opera houses to rat infested subways, where the unwanted and forgotten citizens of NY and other States sleep in urine infested passageways along with rats and other denizens of the underground continued their onerous lives in a state of deep denial. "Greatest City in the World," they say.

About to get worse. Cleaner, but worse. "Cleaner" because no "human refuse" is tolerated there, and the disabled disappear by the thousands from the residential hospitals right under the noses of the carefully selected, hand-picked, screened and vetted denizens of Alinsky Island, the great experiment in the "deconstruction" of the Constitutional USA.

And no, a cursory search online will reveal no reference to Columbia U School of Sociology and the role it played in this experiment.

It was pretty at first, and attractive – many wild open spaces, rare birds, according to Fr Pershe, SJ, an amateur ornithologist and former, kindly, chaplain at Coler Hospital; pheasants ran wild in the quieter corners, wild and unusual plants abounded, and the disabled from either end of the residential hospitals could wheel or walk through the small roads and pathways in perfect safety and freedom.

Until Nelson Rockefeller broke ground on a new project, a community outside the Constitution of the USA, a community governed by appointed "executives," a community united on one side of the "Maginot Line" and horrendously divided on the other, in the name of "multiculturalism," the catch cry of the "divide and conquer" system passed on from one tyrant to another. Columbia University's School of Sociology, designed the experiment, monitored and after three decades, closed it as Obama somehow took the President's seat in the Oval Office, and expanded the experiment all over the nation.

As pretty as it was, I only intended to stay for two years.

Instead, was trapped for thirty. Every time I got close to leaving, the drawbridge slammed shut. There was *constant, relentless,* interference in my life and that of my children; sabotage of work, social life, endeavours, professional life, etc., *ad nauseum.*

There was no privacy. There was no real friendship. Everyone could see if you were dressed for work or casually. In order to move around normally I learned to "down dress." If I dressed in any way professional or festively or elegantly I would be literally "blockaded" on Main Street as one person after another would approach to tell me how well I looked and try to discover where I was going and why, etc. A walk that took under ten minutes would end up taking thirty. If I didn't stop and talk to them, there would be "what's wrong with her?" followed by consequences, phone calls: "You didn't say hello to me today..."

"And who, pray tell, are you!"

Note that majority of such persons wouldn't bother giving a nod or hello on most days.

At first I considered such intrusions to be petty, stupid, gossip oriented.

Then as I noted one bizarre incident after another in my places of work I realised there was something deeper and more sinister.

All roads led back to the Lenox Hill Democrat Club enforcer, aka the "silverback," for her aggressive stance and prowling up and down the halls attempting to intimidate me. For expedience, she is aka as RF or the "Enforcer."

There cannot be peace, joy, creativity, economic success, growth, where there is such a preponderance of abortion culture. The mother who *coldly decides to murder her child will have no compunction about extending that betrayal to other friendships.*

There are mothers who anguish over abortion but still go inside to those houses of horror and baby slaughter. From what I have observed over the years, i.e., young women sobbing their eyes out because they want to keep their babies, *most* abortions are *coerced.* No "choice" at all!

On Alinsky Island the mothers were married or in stable relationships but, *the majority of women known personally to me,* chose to murder their second or third child. To some it was a "Rite of Passage." I only knew two other women who had not had an abortion. They were also from Europe.

Grandmothers were also culpable, one of the most disturbing being a plump, nondescript woman who had sacrificed her 8 year old daughter to sa*an and subjected her to the most vile experiences. Needless to say the child was confined in a mental institution for years then released into the 'nice safe Island" aka the NY Gulag.

She didn't stand a chance. Forced into a third abortion by her mother and psychiatrist, she lost her moment of freedom and independence and disappeared from the Island, presumably back to the mental hospital. She tried to escape her mother, but the control was too strong, too intense. She might have had a chance *anywhere else but Helltown.*

Another young woman, raped by her brother in law, was forced to abort the baby by her own father. She had three more pregnancies. Her father forced her to abort the babies, but she deceived him with the fifth and now has a healthy brood.

Her mother aborted her first child and constantly abandoned the subsequent children before returning to abandon them again.

The Alinsky playbook was embedded from the start:

Cut off the support network and isolate the target from sympathy. Go after people and not institutions; people hurt faster than institutions." Saul Alinsky

And to think a significant number of Americans wanted a woman who idolised this concept to be their President! And yes, she launched her Presidential bid from the Alinsky Gulag, the "second home" of George Soros, Nazi collaborator, specialist in economic warfare and political manipulation, and ruthless neighbour of the Clintons of Chappaqua.

Hillary's cohorts are not her friends. They *have zero respect* for the traitor but have used her in every way possible. No sympathy, however. Her greed and lust for power was her consent, and her rabid hatred for the innocent pre-natal infants will be her forever downfall.

May God have mercy on her cruel, sadistic, soul.

SOVIET PLANS FOR THE DESTRUCTION OF THE CHRISTIAN WEST.

1. Yuri Bezmenov, ex KGB: "ideological subversion would change the perception of reality of every American. And the individualist culture of the West.
2. The subversion would start slowly, thus:
3. Demoralisation (covert, 15-50 years) Basically completed.
4. Destabilizastion (overt, 2-5 years)
5. Crisis (6 weeks)
6. Violent Change and Normalisation (years to infinity)
7. How it worked on the Gulag:
8. Lure naïve Kool Aid drinkers and innocents to an isolated island. Tell them it is Utopia, Paradise, then stealthily remove all assets, eg, wild flowers, birds, transport, and bring on a significant percentage of disturbed persons to teach and criminals in uniform to control decent folk...until the independently wealthy leave and the vulnerable original residents are trapped as experimental "subjects" in a town also called HELL.
9. Remove the rent subsidies and quadruple the rent.
10. Suddenly quadruple rents and start evicting and threaten with eviction when tenants cannot pay a sudden $4,000 extra per month.
11. Disperse all previous tenants, drive to nervous breakdowns, by harassment, violence, false charges, until all witnesses to the process are driven away, and then spread the program across the USA.

Hence America under Obama. An extension of the experiment.
But with one major error.
Which you'll have to figure out for yourselves!

"THE TRAM I AM…"

"I am the tram. The tram I am."

Seriously! That was the slogan chanted by the brainwashed denizens of the Isle of Woe in opposition to an attempt to paint the second cabin blue as a safety precaution.

In an emergency, saying to Emergency workers – go to "the blue cabin" as opposed to "*the red cabin on the South side moving West…*" would appear to be strongly advantageous to the safety of the passengers.

But not to the Alinsky-ites living comfortable bureaucratic lives at the expense of taxpayers in NY or around the world.

They wanted both tram cabins to be red, because red was the colour of the sociological concoction known officially as Roosevelt Island, designed, constructed and managed by the NWO "Usual Suspects," at the time the colour of Communism, *Krasnaya Ploched!*

Confusion, Chaos and hardship were the embedded conditions of life there.

Isolation from mainstream America and the media were ancillary precautions for the continuation of the experiment.

Access was by a tin box on a wheelie wire, i.e. an aerial tram way between Manhattan and the Gulag. Such tramways are in use at ski resorts and isolate mountain areas. They were never designed for heavy commuter use.

They were freezing in winter and broiling in summer. Heaters were added, *overhead,* to serve only the tallest. Top of head, barely warm – feet and nether regions freezing.

The tram kept breaking down.

The tram frequently went off between 10am and 3 pm, i.e., serving the bureaucrat and student population while making life hell for free lancers and artists with flexible hours.

The tram didn't function during storms, blizzards or when they didn't feel like providing transport.

During one very cold day, sub-zero temperature, when they decided to leave us stranded on the tower in Manhattan for an hour, I had to point out to them that the disabled population could die from hypothermia, or lose a foot or hand or nose, because they could not move their bodies to generate heat. The "mechanically impaired" tram was suddenly functioning again.

Initially, residents had priority on the tram – not a problem on normal days, but essential on the crowded nightmare of, say, the Fourth of July. Some charming liberal challenged that rule, proclaiming an "equal right" to use the tram, so that hundreds of residents, including seniors and disabled, were delayed taking their meds or returning to their children, families, etc., leaving children waiting outside their doors, or wandering off, at high risk from the "carefully screened" perverts and lunatics aka Public Safety or neighbours. More on that later. And yes, the majority of residents were "on meds."

If you were not a UN diplomat, or a Democrat Party apparatchik, your professional life was toast.

The tram was met by electric buses that kept breaking down. If you were carrying packages or not in a condition to walk, you were stuck on a tiny bus at the mercy of the crudest and rudest people in New York, and if you already had to deal with them on the tram, that constituted approximately 30 minutes of abuse. Each way.

They would remain quiet while blacks blasted their boom box, but shout me down if I asked them to turn it down. Notices were posted on the bus forbidding the playing of electronic equipment, but the driver was silent. Left wingers are cowards. Most drivers and entry level workers, e.g., nurses' aides, RIPS got their jobs through connections with the East Harlem or Lenox Hill Democrat Clubs. Occasionally a normal person slipped through the cracks.

One such was the mini bus driver from Guyana, not impressed by the rudeness that he witnessed on the job. I knew I was safe if he were driving. He was of East Indian extract, discreet but clearly not well impressed at what he saw of the so called "Americans" on Isle of Woe, the "safest" place to live in NY!!!

"Safe" – as in the well-dressed woman from the privately owned apartments who tried to bully me into leaving my seat across from her so that she could place her packages on them. Very upset when I refused. Clearly medicated. The seats on either side of her were vacant!

After a bizarre call in the early days from a man I knew only by sight, I learned to smile and say hello to everyone, Queen Mother style, to "humour the inmates."

One called and complained that I "did not say hello to (him) on the minibus..."

Er "Who are you?"

Sometimes I had to make 20 greetings between my apartment door and the path past the maintenance workers office. The path was shy of 100 yards!

God help those poor men – having to deal with the "inmates" of the open air, minimum security nuthouse!

Their supervisor, Woody, played a major role in saving my life in 2006. May have been fired for it, material witness so to speak.

More on the social interactions later.

I have good reason to believe that I encountered the Central Park Murderer on the tram.

Helen the liberal white house correspondent – told me as we were boarding the bus that she had never seen anything like that. She moved soon afterward. She was left-wing, but honest.

On another occasion there was one seat left on the bus. It was in a row of two, but a burly black male occupied both, his legs spread wide open.

I asked him if he would make room for me to sit down.

He made eye contact with the other passengers, who obviously knew him and smirked.

"There's no room," he said.

"There will be if you move your knees together," I replied.

"Well I have something between *my* legs!"

Seriously!

I later encountered this donkey's derriere when I reported the attempts on my life by RIPS. An idiot. A *lawyer* hired by New York State! Kind of explains a thing or three. He did not have the gravitas of a Ben Carson, or

Thomas Sowell, and seemed stuck at "frat boy" getting a free "colour of skin" pass through professional school. Affirmative Action and EOE as rewards for skin colour and not for achievement are ultimately a disservice to minority students and taxpayer alike.

He was a lawyer for RIOC, obviously hired both for the colour of his skin and the sleazy content of his character.

Stephen Shane, a later President of RIOC and lawyer, was also disgusting. Although the Director of Security was on leave the day of the first attempt on my life, and not complicit, Shane called him in to "meet with me."

Shane was cynical, and disgusting, and it was pathetic to see the Director of Security kissing up and pleading for his job.

He grovelled so much I didn't have a chance to say that the RIPS goons took advantage of his day off to commit his crimes.

Although he seemed sometimes slightly tipsy, and I surmised from his addiction to lotto tickets that he was in debt, and while I really detested the "Yo' lookin' mighty fine today" with the up and down look, when push came to shove with the vicious bunch of thugs that he inherited, he always did the right thing and kept them in line as much as possible, given that they were all protégés of the DemRat Party, handpicked by RF, aka the "silverback," and he had little real power or control.

And before you scream "racist," I also applied that term to Angela Merkel for her bizarre posturing and belligerence toward President Trump.

He fit right in, but interestingly, was one of the first to face the firing line once the assault and the failure to make me disappear rippled upward. He, too, was "disappeared" from the Isle of Loons.

Black America – the Dems "ain't yo'" friends!

You're the fail safes, the "throw downs," the scapegoats.

NWO Democrats will cannibalise you, too, if you refuse their Kool Aid.

They were already cannibalising their own children – selling baby organs to transplant and tissues to skin care and food flavouring.

Wondering how motor neuron disease is now ubiquitous rather than rare?

Some "credit" of course, must go to the injurious and destructive Vaccine Injury "industry.'

However, let us not forget that those who devour human flesh in one form or another are at extremely high risk for kuru kuru or "cannibal's disease."

Symptoms are very similar to those manifest by Hillary Clinton on the campaign trail.

XVII

PS 217 CRIME SCENE and RIPS – NY State Sponsored Perverts and felons.

The elementary school was divided among several buildings. The much vaunted Principal, Charlotte somebody was injured before the school opened, and so the school was leaderless for the first year.

Children were molested in the school. From the very beginning. Little girls as young as 6 were followed into the rest rooms and molested or raped.

True to Alinsky's "khaos" style, there was no security in the school. Anyone could walk in and out – or lurk and hide.

Most of the teachers appeared medicated one way or another. The school guidance counsellors appeared to be selected from the minions of Hell.

"I hear you say you *want your child to read.*"

"I don't know how you heard that. I said my child *can read; books, time from an analogue clock and make mathematical calculations in her head without prompting.*"

"I hear you say you *want* your child to read."

"I told you, she can already read."

"Well, I don't know that."

"Then test her."

"We can't do that."

Maria Schianni, referred to by an Italian American friend as a "Sicilian loudmouth" knew very well that the LAW required her to test my daughter within 90 days. I saw nothing Italian in her character.

This was the same party who told two parents to "smoke pot with your son..." when they expressed concern about his addiction and the source of his supply.

The parents later divorced. The mother was taken out in handcuffs and charged with drug trafficking – their son ordered a Fed Ex package full of marijuana, which the unwitting mother innocently accepted. The son later died tragically of ALS – Lou Gehrig's disease, aka Amniotrophic Lateral Sclerosis – a terrible disease.

There was a hotline to the Psych department of New York Hospital and a shuttlebus between the Hospital and the Island – the one thing that worked. Irony – or strategy?

Children were kidnapped from the playground. Two seven year old girls abducted by a 14 year old sex offender from across the Bridge. Note, at the time there were security officers on duty in a booth on the bridge at all times. "Jane and Jenny" were passed by a Nassau Co Cop who lived on the Island. This cop knew them both – they played with his own girls, but he did not pause to question their presence in a concrete parking garage with a complete stranger.

Turned out that said cop was a coke head and drug dealer, with other crimes to his name. He had 12 residences in three years, yet the "extreme vetting" did not flag a potential, serious problem, i.e., cocaine use and dealing with its attendant problems of bankruptcy, chaos and negligence. Took an entire family hostage and got away with it.

Then again, he claimed to be part Native American, so was held to a different standard.

Children were attacked by black gangs coming in from Queens. Tony Capobianco organised defences – every baseball bat in the Gulag was requisitioned for the defensive army that met them at the entrance to the bridge. They retreated without a skirmish.

A couple committed murder suicide.

More suicides.

Another murder suicide.

A disabled couple who had lived happily in Coler or Goldwater for many years could not cope with the stresses and abuse on Utopian Island. First the wife defenestrated, then the husband. I didn't know the wife but the man, "Jake" was a warm, friendly man, kind and outgoing, with none of the political nonsense imported from the Lenox Hill and East Harlem DemRat Club Members. They moved in from the hospitals.

Teenagers were raped. Some, allegedly, by Public Safety. They told friends, never parents.

They were all terrified of Public Safety. Some claimed that teenagers were raped by Public Safety but they were too terrified to report them to their parents or police.

A teenager defenestrated in the presence of Public Safety.

Children and teenagers were molested and raped by the notorious outfit aka Roosevelt Island Public Safety.

Many disappeared.

Public Safety – RIPS - appears to have had a deal with Ruger and Fellaria of the FDNY's EMS Unit to abduct their targets.

From a disturbing personal experience and narrow escape from Public Safety, (DG) I have no doubt that the disappeared teenagers were raped in the ambulances and then murdered.

Not a word in the media. Not a word to the community.

It was a "crime free," "gun free" Island.

And no matter how many persons died violently, it would remain the perfect "gun free" utopia in the eyes of the residents and public. Yet, they are infiltrating PDs around the nation.

One of their former "recruits" the token white, was arrested for shooting indiscriminately out of the windows of his Stuyvesant Town Apartment – after being recruited by the NYPD. They can go straight into NYPD Sergeant status after spending a few years terrorising residents and visitors alike.

Until of course, 600 families were deviously and illicitly displaced once the "experiment" was over. 1974 to 2004.

The strategy of disposing of undesirables is revoltingly similar to that relative to the disappearance of Theresa Heinz Kerry. Last seen as an unidentifiable body in a gurney being wheeled into an ambulance; then some footage of ambo on its way to airport, allegedly to Boston Airport. Then complete news blackout for ... 10 years...?

Stalin is alive and well and living in Dem'rat America!

"Denial" is one side effect of the Liberal Kool Aid. The brainwashed liberals could witness the most appalling events, violent crimes such as assault and battery, abduction, drug dealing, a series of missing teenagers and still convince themselves that Roosevelt Island was the "safest place to live in the USA."

My primary suspects for the missing teenagers are members or former members of the Roosevelt Island Public Safety. *One RIPS kreep was sentenced in N. Carolina for attempting to lure minors to the bathroom in McDonalds.*

My primary suspect for the "uniformed cop" raping women at the 21st Street subway, and committing burglaries in the area are also Roosevelt Island Public Safety – RIPS! As in RIPS DECENCY AND LAW TO SHREDS.

One Director after another was leveraged out after crimes by the low level "ossifers," those hired through the Lenox Hill Demrat Club cartel. The Directors of Public Safety were mostly political appointees, donors to the Party, former Housing Police Lieutenants for example, guys who never made Captain, but the thugs on the street were just that – thugs and minions.

Yet after three weeks "training," they received powers almost equal to the NYPD, who then had to check in first with them and follow their instructions on the Loony Toons Island and also be made accountable for the multiple mistakes, falsehoods, lies and errors of Public Safety if a case ever came to court.

Usually by the time the NYPD would arrive, the victims would be so disgusted they just wanted to forget about the Hell that those New York State RIPS employees had put them through and dropped charges.

Where Public Safety were the criminals, they had the advantage. The NYPD had to check in with them first, took the first "briefings" from them and were thereby prejudiced and misled in almost every situation.

Even so, an NYPD officer stated off the record that *"Most of the problems on Roosevelt Island were caused by Public Safety."* His partner concurred. More details and factual accounts in further chapters, but doesn't it cheer the taxpayers' heart to know that at least $9 *million per year* was spent maintaining this gang of racist thugs and paying them as much, if not more than the highly trained professionals at the NYPD!

The 114th were mostly really great, amazing Police Officers who somehow maintained their integrity despite a tsunami of corruption from one "City Hall" after another, and particularly in the unmonitored, unsupervised, politically correct, multiculti insanity on Alinsky Island.

Again, the uniformed goons ran the place; the residents had no authentic police protections and took the RIPS on trust. Few thought to call the NYPD unless there was severe violence, and then investigations would be short-circuited by the RIPS goons.

<u>Known crimes by RIPS</u>

- Assault and battery of innocent civilians. Multiple counts.
- Arrest on false charges. Multiple accounts.
- Kidnapping, battery and molestation of a minor. Multiple counts.
- Colour of Law Abuses – multiple counts.
- Racist (anti-white) discrimination in cases of harassment and assault. Multiple counts.
- Collusion in the commission of a crime. Multiple counts.
- Kidnapping, attempted abduction, sexual molestation of a civilian.

- Conspiracy to commit murder, collusion with rogue EMTs, FDNY.
- Attempted murder.
- Lying to the NYPD – multiple counts.
- Rapes of minors – alleged, multiple counts.

Probable collusion in the disappearances of teenagers – multiple counts.

At least North Carolina knew how to handle these creeps – one, Cesar (aka Wilson) Toro was arrested, indicted and convicted of attempting to procure sex from minors in a McDonald's in NC. He received a custodial sentence. Primary suspect for the 21st subway rapes.

In an attempted cover up of the attempts on my life by him and others, Toro was fired, eventually.

The Director of Public Safety was fired. He was the least guilty. They chose his day off to make their worst harassments - including the two attempts on my life. Watching this black police lieutenant crawl and beg Stephen Shane to keep his job was shocking.

Another Director of Public Safety, Keith Guerrero was fired. Molester "Detective" Seftkakis fired.

One President of RIOC, Herbert Berman was fired after the tram was hit by lightning and his utter incompetence was exposed. He quit. Got the Divine message, loud and clear!

Herbert was the President of RIOC at the time of the two attempts on my life by RIPS. He refused to take any action, told me to talk to Paul Harte, an Affirmative Action employee and law school graduate (alleged). The same person whom I previously encountered on the mini bus who refused to move his leg to let me sit down because he had "something between his legs…"

Another President of RIOC, Stephen Shane, was publicly removed from a meeting and fired after my report of the attempts on my life reached one of the Roosevelt Island websites. However, there was no attempt to reach out, compensate or provide Victim Services to me or my family.

I have no doubt that they will claim there was "no connection."

It was challenged by one of the nutters, possible Dick Lutz, editor of the Main Street WIRE, aka 'The Liar"- which was highly selective in its reporting of the events on the Island.

I called Dick Lutz on my return from the hospital after the first attempt, and he reluctantly agreed to meet me in the lobby of Rivercross, the Move on.org HQ, and New York State subsidised co-op.

Prowling in the background was Ellen, his advertising manager, a sweet women, but clueless. It appeared that big Dick was afraid of me, and wanted not only the protection of the doorman but of this diminutive inoffensive woman. Typical liberal coward – "Big Dick" hiding behind a little woman!

He was highly evasive and clearly not in the least interested in knowing that RIPS were abducting citizens from Main Street and using EMS Ambulance for intended rape and murder. Which leads me to question whether he was partisan to this in any way. He was definitely part of the "program" – leaving a lucrative job in London to run a "community newspaper" for 5,000 residents????

The "community newspaper" notoriously and shamelessly promoted one of its publishers for School Principal, Dorothy Bowser, another, Dr Resnick, as the solution for Obama's new health care project, etc., etc. Dr Resnick made house-calls to the seniors. Noble or Sinister? Shameless! There is no longer a "Seniors' building."

All this must sound very bizarre to normal people who have never lived in a totalitarian state, or a proto totalitarian community designed to study the most effective means of de-Constitutionalising the USA, but Dick Lutz had abundant other reports of RIPS abuses which he suppressed. He had no excuse – he chose to be part of the problem, not the solution. He also wrote a puff piece on RF faking the name of her slasher granddaughter.

Then again, the "LIAR" was not a newspaper, per se, but an instrument of agit-prop, registered in Virginia!

The most poignant of all the RIOC Presidents who did not complete terms of office was Dr Jerome Blue. He was Christian, Conservative, intelligent, and a gentleman – but worse than all, black!

That is, he was a black who escaped the mind control plantation run by the Democrat-Communist Party.

The Soviets had an indoctrination centre in Moscow called the Patrice Lumumba University. It was created to bring Africans and American "negroes" together to create divisions and conflict in their home countries and so bring about Communist revolutions.

Louis Armstrong, Paul Robeson, were alleged to be graduates of Lumumba, which now functions as the "International University," but its subversive work continues in the virtual Plantation called the Democrat Party.

Every member of Congress, every elected official who has been there must admit it immediately.

It is highly likely that Willy Clinton fled there after accusations of rape at Oxford U. It is established that he spent three weeks in Moscow around that time. He's certainly got the "dialectic" down!

Dr Blue was accused of shutting the Islanders out. A blatant lie. He opened the door to Island Residents, for weekly meetings – the only President of RIOC ever to so do.

He tried to help small business – mostly blacks opened up new businesses on the previously empty store fronts.

He nominated me to Governor Pataki's Board. That generated a fire storm of hate calls from the "Enforcer" and her cabal to Albany, calling me a "racist," etc. Yet on the Island only three people knew – Dr Blue, myself and Dr Blue's closest aid, Michael G., an ethical gentleman, also ditched. Needless to say I never sat on the Board.

Blue generated strong interest from the Marriott Group, in building a hotel, along with water taxis, job training for the Island youth, etc., on the South end of the Island.

For this he and his aides were excoriated, vilified, and hounded by the despicable Main Street Wire, editors and publisher alike.

They wanted their shrine to the father of American communism – Franklin Delano Roosevelt and his cousin and wife or "beard," Eleanor.

Finally they did a "Clarence Thomas" on Dr. Blue and accused him of sexual harassment.

Dr Blue had impeccable manners. There are very few men in NY with whom I would sit in a closed room. Donald Trump is one. Dr Blue was another. Ambassador Curley yet another.

It is usually liberal wimps who are sleazy – not red blooded gentleman.

Dr. Blue was accused of sexual harassment, then when that didn't stick, "gender differentiation" for holding the door for a female receptionist, "Tammy." That female receptionist was part of the swamp, the link to the Silverback, RF, aka the "enforcer."

Tammy received a generous settlement. No doubt by pre-arrangement with a Rat Party judge like Eileen Rakower, one of the most corrupt and evil women on the planet.

Governor Pataki appointed Dr Blue Human Rights Commissioner for New York State. Took a couple of months but the Valkyries of the left pushed him out of that job, and then out of a subsequent teaching job in one of the colleges.

You can't fight City Hall when the corrupt Dems are in charge.

What's destroying a life and career to monsters invested in the sadistic slaughter of pre-natal infants!

LGBT man-hater, Judge Eileen Rakower, is notorious in Chinatown. I saw many signs from people she treated unjustly posted on the streets.

She also sent a young man to Riker's Island on Christmas Eve. His crime? Arriving a few minutes late to her court for assignment of a public defender.

Why did he need a defender? Because he was defending himself from a man who a few months previously had attacked him with a machete causing serious injuries. This man was an illegal alien from Columbia, released on his own recognisance that very night.

The young defendant obtained an Order of Protection against the Columbian, but this was ignored by the thugs at Roosevelt Island Public "Safety" (RIPS) who insisted that the NYPD arrest both when Guzman attacked him again.

Under the direction of the Lenox Hill Democrat Club Officer and Board of Elections Local Co-ordinator, RIPS made sure his young victim could not walk freely on the Gulag, nor use the subway, by harassing him themselves, or assuring that the island gangs could pursue and assault him.

In order to arrive at Rakower's Court in Chinatown, he had to take two tedious buses, wait for the second one to arrive, then take a subway, for a journey of almost two hours. The direct subway journey? 20-30 minutes. No doubt man-hater Rakower was hand-picked for the case, ensuring maximum spite and hatred toward the handsome young male.

He eventually became a refugee from the nation of his birth, the USA.

As did I.

XVIII

Stalin's Revenge – EDUCATION as INDOCTRINATION

With a few rare and blessed exceptions, teachers on the Gulag appeared personally selected for psychopathic or sociopathic tendencies. By God's grace, some saints filtered through, like light dappling darkened leaves. Miss Isabel Stern and Michael Rosenberg were outstanding. Miss Lewis, who didn't quite get everything, and lived in five seasons was otherwise kind and supportive. Most of the others were sociopaths, psychos or suffered from Post Abortion Syndrome. They cared nothing for the children in their care, not safety, not education, not character.

Did the PS IS 217 HR questionnaire included such questions as:

- Do you hate kids?
- Do you have Post Abortion Syndrome?
- Have you read "Rules for Radicals?"
- Was Stalin an effective educator?
- Do all male children suffer from ADD or ADHD?
- Should boys be taught to get in touch with their feminine side?
- Should mediocrity be encouraged as a long term globalist goal?
- Do you believe in giving children a psych diagnosis as early as possible?

If the answer was "Yes" to all of the above, they received an assignment in the "easiest school" in Manhattan.

That's the way I see it – may never have happened but certainly fits the picture.

And so, into the Gulag marched an army of sick and twisted women with an agenda. Again, there were a number of exceptions – teachers outstanding in dedication and integrity, despite being vastly outnumbered by the freaks whom I will call Esels. I do not know how the few decent teachers, the "resistance" could bear to work alongside the Esels.

Esel sind eindeutig eine Spezies, Art für sich. You're going to have to look that up yourselves. It's my little private joke! Hint – an Esel brays.

One, Mrs "Grossesel" systematically bullied a brilliant child into believing he could not do math. That child's hobby was designing aeroplanes, jets, machinery, etc. He was brilliant, a superfast learner from a family of scientists, and even in his adult years is still too discouraged to even attempt what he once learned so easily outside her classroom before she shattered his self-confidence and set him up as a target for bullying. Her name was Mrs. Brown.

Grossesel also sent vulnerable 8 year old girls to the deli for her bagels, putting them at risk of kidnapping in an island with a recent, harrowing history of the abduction of 7, 8 year old girls. There were molestations, assaults and attempted rapes in the school bathrooms.

Another teacher, Krankesel, swore openly at the children, smoked in the classroom, tried to sell jewellery to the parents and lied about any parent who dared to criticise her. Her uncle later became school Principal, so we were stuck with her despite numerous complaints over many years. She was bragging about "cusinaire rods" for teaching fractions, and was highly offended when I advised her my 5 year old daughter was already computing percentages and teaching herself long division. Math is easy for some kids when you add a dollar sign to the numbers! In Junior High my daughter was in the top 2% of national Math scholars. The school did not tell her about the Math Honor Society, and I knew nothing about it, being from England. "Ethnic" kids in the 15th percentile were advised to join. But the teachers on Crazy Island were not like the teachers I knew from England, who loved bright children – or indeed, just loved children and nurtured and respected each according to his or her abilities.

That was *not* Helen Shepherd, whose very name invokes the Biblical admonition – "Woe to the Shepherd who scatters the sheep…" This "Shepherd" threw her charges over the cliff and to the wolves.

Oddly enough I encountered a teacher from England, on some professional visit or exchange, and she confided identical concerns after a very brief visit to the school. Like me, she "could not believe" what she witnessed at the school.

Unlike me, she could go home. She was not economically trapped in a "utopian" ghetto, next to an enemy who wanted her to disappear off the face of the earth but was so stupid as to do everything in her power to sabotage her escape.

The principal, Solomon Zeichner, was such a disaster that an Associate Principal named Harry Milner was appointed to "assist" him.

Harry had degrees from a top University in Ireland, a Masters in Education, and a Degree in Music from Birmingham and had worked with the famed Halle Orchestra. He also loved and cared for children.

Not only did the school scores start to soar, but in a matter of months he developed a National class school choir.

Did they appoint Milner Principal when the creepy Zeichner left? No!

The same "Main Street Wire," aka "The Liar," praised the *Milner* improved scores on its front page while its own editor *also* wrote and published personal letters and hostile editorials excoriating Harry Milner alongside articles gushing praise and adulation for the horrendous failure and dishonest creep, Solomon Zeichner.

There was a public meeting. In true Commie-Dem'rat style, anyone who tried to speak for Harry Milner was shouted down. That would be one person – me. The rest had been told that Dorothy Bowser was already in play as the next Principal. Liberal sycophancy on steroids. Kool Aid kolkhoz!

The only place that I previously witnessed such vulgarity was at "Speakers Corner" in Hyde Park as a very young child.

Shortly after this meeting, the wife of the founding publisher of the WIRE, Dorothy Bowser, was appointed as Principal of PS 217. Two years later she resigned, with an enhanced pension and retirement package based on her elevated Principal's salary, while the work and accomplishments of dedicated Harry Milner were completely reversed.

Bowser wasn't the worst, but she was a dyed-in-the wool Dem'rat invested in status and taxpayer funded retirement benefits. They were already extremely well off, despite her drab, Marxist 101 appearance.

Harry had three strikes against him: First, he was Irish, secondly, he had high standards but worst of all, he loved and cared for the children, neither of which attributes were readily applied to either Zeichner or Bowser.

To culture-starved children, he organised a choir, which, within a year had become national class.

But as with Dr Blue, he was hounded out of office by the perfidious, pernicious, insidious publishers of the Main Street WIRE, id est, LIAR.

And now, it can serve as the prototype for left wing news services across the nation – the original beat-down of a good man, hide the truth, far left, agenda driven, FAKE NEWS.

Free Kool Aid with each copy!

XIX

DRUGS DRUGS DRUGS

It was often inferred as well as stated "as fact," that Roosevelt Island was also planned as a locus for drug distribution to the five boroughs.

Drug use were almost *de rigeur* there – from the elegant stockbroker's wife using "recreational" cocaine to the drug addicted prostitute daughter of RF, later to die from AIDS, to the Greek brothers dealing directly out of the "Green Kitchen"/ "Trellis," to the Mafia Moll turned CCD Teacher's son with an arsenal of guns and cocaine under his bed, to the white limousine that would pull up outside the co-op building, Rivercross, home to the more prosperous Democrat donors, and thence to the last phase – a giant black Humvee with the "Black Moslems" – black men with stocking caps and barely concealed weapons establishing their presence every so often, weekly.

The primary targets for sale of these vile substances was white, middle class children and teenagers. They had *entrée* into places where blacks would still be suspect at that time, and so could expand the drug markets.

The plan was to turn them into dealers and to turn the white girls into 'hos.' In the later years it was sickening to see how well that plan had succeeded, as young black thugs walked around with a posse of young white teenagers, as young as 12. They would address them as "yo bitch," or "you hos" and treat them with the contempt they had acquired from watching decades of movies and television shows where the black man or, usually woman, was the more intelligent and resourceful of the plotline and the whites were contemptible, stupid, slow witted or evil starting with "Roots." "White Men Can't Jump" Was the title of one movie – seriously!

The Bill Cosby show, had few white characters. Since I watched it rarely, the only white characters that I personally observed were two or three "white trash" girls in a cabin – in Chicago yet! – trying to get the pristine black teens drunk.

The other white character that I observed in Bill Cosby's racist "Cosby Show" was an obese white car salesman in a garish plaid jacket.

Nothing racist there. Just an attempt to create a score-keeping stereotype!

The apartment assigned to us was in the only enclosed floor in a building that was supposed to be an "afterthought." The giant Eastwood complex was a rabbit warren, which also facilitated drug dealing. You could go into one door at the North end of the street and come out another door six blocks at the South end of the street, and, indeed, exit by multiple entrances in between – North, South, East *and* West.

Very secure.

Not.

Disastrous for parents and parenting. An "open border!" More later.

My special, secure, "elite" floor was intended exclusively for black or Hispanic Democrats, and almost every apartment had a substance abuse problem.

My late husband was a JFK Democrat. I was a Conservative Republican, with a reference from

Ambassador Curley, President Ford's Ambassador to Ireland, and Reagan's Ambassador to France. He invited us there. It was a completely different America. Having a reference from Ambassador Curley would have been an asset, but once the Rats controlling the Island got wind of it, the knives were out even before I moved in. Back to the drugs.

The first apartment on that "exclusive" floor was occupied by a white family. However, they were whites serving blacks on behalf of the City of NY, i.e. teaching black ex-cons how to establish small businesses. Generously subsidised. Many of the teenagers were drug users and rehearsed their rock band all day Saturday and at night it was like living above a piano bar. One of the young men was talented but afraid to perform in public. I gave him an opportunity to play at my dance recital. From their point of view he was doing *me* the favour. Yes it was lovely and he was actually the nicest of the lot, and certainly an enhancement, but not absolutely essential. His degree was in Mathematics. His living was by doing the work he loved most – playing the piano, and he was in constant demand, bless him. The one "clean and sober" member of the family.

The next apartment was inhabited by the most vicious human being on the planet. Some other tenants nicknamed her "the missing link" and the "silverback." I'll just call her "RF" Her patrolling and posturing earned her those titles, not her skin colour. I have used similar references for a white bully, Angela Merkel. I go by behaviour, and RF's was as nasty as nasty could be. Definitely tipped off about our arrival and connections, by RIHM, most likely Thelma McIntosh, who unlawfully, illegally, and without any cause, threatened me and my son with homelessness. She was transferred after my complaints, but the hate continued.

RF, miserable creature, waited outside her apartment to "welcome" us with HATE when we first moved our belongings in. She hated my little son, a beautiful, enchanting baby of six months, the envied "white male," on sight, and placed an ill-spelled note in pencil to the effect that we were not wanted there. I found it under my door, the first morning on Loony Tunes Island. A woman with the literacy level of a First Grader handed huge power by the Rat Party.

RF was the "Local Co-ordinator" for the Board of Elections - that would be another word for thug or enforcer, and an "ossifer" of the Lenox Hill Democrat Club. She was deeply connected to the East Harlem Democrats as well.

Her daughter, "Keisha," a drug addicted prostitute, lived with her, along with *her* 6 year old daughter, "Taisha" who was hit by a car and sustained a Traumatic Brain Injury at the age of three while crossing the road with her drug addled mother.

"Taisha" was the only child that I have ever known who was expelled from kindergarten. She was belligerent, but worse for the liberals, she taught the other children how to spell – F-U-C-K.

"Taisha" received an insurance award to be accessed on attaining her majority, i.e. reaching the age of 18, which provided considerable incentive for "RF" to fight for custody of her grand-daughter.

In her teens, Taisha ended up incarcerated for attempting to stab a teenage male to death in a jealous, daylight rage over his attentions to a pretty young Hispanic girl, Sylvia.

On release from jail for the infliction of multiple stab wounds, she claimed to have been in college.   RF

Silverback used her Party influence to change her name and get her training at NYU and employment as a *surgical assistant* at Goldwater Hospital.

RIPS were considerably occupied persuading the NYPD not to bring charges of burglary, armed robbery, assault, perjury, false charges, etc., against this aggressive but pathetic woman

"Keisha," the drug addicted prostitute, mother of "Taisha," was actually the nicest of that family, although she would go into my apartment in my absence and items would disappear. Needless to say, in the Alinsky style of building, most doors there could be opened with a swipe of a credit card.

"Keisha" died of AIDS.

"Lasciate Ogni Speranza, voi ch'entrate" should be emblazoned on the side of every tram and train heading to that accursed place, Dante's 9th Circle of Hell... *"Lose all hope you who enter here..."*

Next door to this hive of protected criminal activity was us, the "Innocents Abroad." We only intended to stay two years, to get our bearings, to give the kids some play areas and freedom from the noise and traffic of Manhattan.

In retrospect the noise and traffic were far safer than the insidious hell of Roosevelt Island.

Moving on, on the other side of our apartment was a lovely lady, "Carmen" from the rental office. She was Puerto Rican, friendly, kind, funny - hooked on cocaine, parties and men. One of her sons became a teen heroin dealer, his girlfriend a heroin user. I heard rumors of suicides, but cannot confirm them. "Carmen" died of AIDS.

I cannot say if "Keisha" and "Carmen" made it to their fortieth birthdays.

Next to them was the Cocaine snorting, dealing Long Island cop, with his children and Stepford wife, allegedly a pill head. Hardly surprising given the 14 house moves in 12 months, the constant debt and disappearance of funds, the increasing control by and of her in laws – a strange couple who watched soap operas with their grandchildren and were highly amused when the 8 and 10 year old started acting out a story line and playing "hookers" by the swimming pool. They were also amused when the kids found the grandfather's Playboy and other porn magazines. The grandfather was a police officer on Long Island. He spent his money on women, his wife spent hers on booze. When the son wanted a gun, as a child, the dad would go in uniform and confiscate one from another child.

Then another alcoholic, prescription dependent widow living with her son – late teens or young adult. She committed suicide shortly after moving into to Looney Toons Island, may she rest in peace. She was white, courteous, though too often "oblivious." Very sad.

Next to her, the pot head, a white professional woman, then a lady with cats, and next to her, a musical pot head with a lawyer parent pursued by the infernal revenue service – they must have been Republicans, as they were fairly civil - and next door to him a Cuban family, seemed fairly nice, but the paterfamilias ended up in a residential hospital following a stroke. Needless to say, the residential hospital was not on the Island and his poor wife had to take three buses to bring him food every day as well as care for her children. Not much help for them, but they managed.

Later "replacements" included the son of a Weatherman i.e., domestic terrorist who died in a violent Attica uprising and a young defector from the IDF national service.

His sister worked for Russell Simmons, notorious rap producer, heavily involved in campaigning for Barack Obama and at least the appearances of vote rigging. Handing out pre-paid credit cards to ghetto dwellers the month before an election, combined with heavy fundraising and such, looks just a touch suspicious!

The pot smoking travel agent was replaced by a little Northern Irish grandmother, another left-winger, full of fire and "anti-Brit brimstone" – yet somehow we became, em, cautious friends, appreciating and standing by one another, without either trusting the other. Her daughter was connected with the Provisional – i.e. fake IRA, a group of upstart but violent terrorists. She was married to a former member of the SDS, Students for a Democratic Society, Mark Rudd, who had become a very wealthy real estate lawyer. They lived in a capacious apartment in Greenwich Village, complete with skylight and such, huge kitchen which could house half a dozen starving actors and a grand piano which no one played, but for which a tutor was hired, and a charming daughter, adored by her grandmother.

They moved grandmother into the nice "safe" Isle of Loons to keep her from her drinking buddies in a still Irish enclave of Queens, the neighboring Borough of NY.

Only problem was, every Wednesday, the feisty gal would toddle over to the oul' neighborhood for a hair do and a chin-wag, catching up on the gossip and later spending her social security check in the pub.

She'd stagger into a taxi, make it safely to Main Street and there weave her way down the path and up the ramp to her apartment, usually losing her key and having to stagger back to find maintenance and the creepy Public Safety to escort her home.

The next couple of days she would be like a basket of cranky crabs, till Friday night one of the daughters would pick her up, feed her, and she'd sober up and make through to the following Wednesday pub "Seisiun" as they call it in Ireland – north and south - and the whole cycle would start again!

It is likely that RIPS were in cahoots with her daughters to "keep an eye" on her, and with RIHM, who profited from a turnover in apartments, because one day the daughters came and moved her to their country home in Massachusetts, far from the pub, far from public transport, far from friends, and no doubt with a locked liquor cabinet.

She died within a month. Final insult – they buried her in a Protestant gravesite.

Detox is not for amateurs.

There was another mother and son, clean except for body building steroids; a Cuban refugee family – husband with a roving eye and salt of the earth wife, who forgave his infidelities and took care of him following the inevitable stroke. Down the line more drugs, alcohol, cocaine, criminality, a self-styled "native American" family, the second on the floor, not necessarily a statistical anomaly when at least one of the "native American" families admitted lying about the matter, then more drunkenness, drugs, cocaine, pot, Puerto Rican teenager in reform camp – belonged to a gang whose initiation required bashing in the heads of random strangers; and a sweet older black lady, "Susan."

Sally was diabetic, and eventually needed the care of a nurse's aide. She did so well with her aide, that the geniuses at Medicaid/Medicare decided she didn't need one, so Susan started to decline again. I was concerned for her and wrote to CBS' journalist Jim Jensen to see if they could help her. Jim Jensen did. That was when journos may have been left wing but they weren't all sleazes.

I don't think I told her about my letter to Jim Jensen – but just said I was delighted she had her aide back.

Sally lived a good couple of years after that, and when she died, she left a memento for every single apartment dweller from that hallway – just a small photo or something simple.

Everyone except me.

Racists come in all colors. As do rats.

Either that, or some other "racist" decided not to pass on the memento meant for me.

Charming lot, Roosevelt Island 'Rats.

Divide and conquer America. All part of the plan.

It seemed as if all the blacks on the Island followed orders from "RF." One woman, also connected with the East Harlem Democrats, Amelia Fuentes, told me she wasn't supposed to speak to me and that "they" were going to kill her.

A month later she was dead.

She had one of the "special" apartments on the Island – hard to describe but absolutely gorgeous in layout with masses of peripheral space. She had potted palms in her open spaces. Although the apartments were larger than Manhattan apartments going for the same rent, there was barely enough space for essentials, let alone potted palms. Obviously had some clout and an inside track, which ultimately proved fatal.

She was a very civil lady. Deserved better. RIP, Amelia.

Another member of the East Harlem Dems was Gwen. I have her surname somewhere. Her mother operated a bordello, fancy name for whorehouse, in Harlem. Gwen was losing her eyesight, whether from the close work that she did on the evening gowns she designed and sequined, or from hereditary or acquired syphilis she wouldn't say.

She said that at night the men would arrive, cops, politicians, black and white, throw their coats and guns on the bed and get busy with the women.

One way to keep "Tammany Hall" blackmailed and under the control of Harlem mobsters! The Italian mafia had an arrangement with them – owned restaurants, nightclubs, etc.

Gwen promised to do the costumes for The Crucible which I foolishly directed there. She produced not one.

Dem'rats do not keep their word. There is no honor in the world of Liberals. None. Then again, for persons who could inflict excruciating agony on a pre-natal baby, or promote the vivisection of the suffering human person in order to use their organs as "spare parts," or inflict chemical violence on the elderly to murder them, what's a word, what's a promise, what is honor?

Just one person helped me in any way in the production – providing bales of hay. They were furious at my casting methods. When someone was right for the role I hired him or her and was spot on my decisions but for the precursors of the snowflakes it was "life or death," and amateurs expect amateur games. Primitive lighting was supplied, but as for the rest, it was barebones, but somehow beautiful.

I hired a young teenager as an "assistant director," which in English professional theatre means keep the real director supplied with tea…and do various other odds and ends.

This young man, Josh M, was the son of a Weatherman, a domestic terrorist incarcerated and killed in the Attica uprising, and tried to take over the rehearsals, constantly interrupting with puerile suggestions such as hanging paper bats from the ceiling.

I eventually had to tell him not to show up at rehearsal, but they still listed him as "assistant director" in the amateur program.

The production was beautiful – using the absence of proper theatre lighting to create a chiaroscuro effect, every angle and every moment was staged to resemble a Rembrandt painting. It worked well, but all that effort was for just one night.

I gave one professional actor a head start in his return to the professional stage after twenty years or so. When he was cast with my "mentor," Maggie Smith, he didn't bother to invite me. He was an angry man, highly offended when I used the word "obfusc" because *he* had never heard of it.

I'd also had to disengage his wife. He recommended her for a role and she read well. Until it came to the first rehearsal. Her main experience was in Am Dram

(Amateur Dramatics) with a group that did mostly, perhaps exclusively, Gilbert and Sullivan.

Every time her line came up, she would step into the middle of the stage and declaim it. Fine for G and S. Defo not for Miller and the dark history of America's Salem witches, guilty or not!

There were a few writers in the Roosevelt Island Players; they formed a group, and kept pestering me to come to a meeting.

Frankly, I had enough of their contentious personalities during rehearsals, and was not in any hurry to encounter them again, especially in someone else's apartment. On the other hand that did offer an escape route, i.e., better than having them to mine.

I once had a tea party, starting at 3pm, invited some friendly neighbors, endured some irate strangers demanding to be invited, but was aghast to find that Americans don't do 3-5pm tea parties. The last guest left at 11pm! At least they were the few cordial and decent people on the Gulag. Although there was no reciprocity and other neighbors ringing the bell demanding to be invited!!! Loonies! But the amateurs from the "Crucible...?" No way! I learned to meet people outside in neutral territory.

Also, I had a beautiful little baby boy that I wanted to spend every moment with and a little girl that was not happy about her new brother and getting adjusted to a new place. The island was distinctly under populated at the time and far from the pizazz of Manhattan which my daughter once enjoyed.

Eventually I agreed to attend a meeting. I asked for orange juice and received a Harvey Wallbanger. Dan, the lead in the Crucible, was a social worker, and I chided him for spiking my drink. If I were an alcoholic in recovery it would be very nasty. He was a bit embarrassed but agreed and apologized; thereafter it was assumed that *I* was an alcoholic in recovery. All the women present took offense. They were American, mostly New Yorkers.

Susan read her play which was about Seniors and incontinence. It was supposed to be a comedy. I suggested it might be a little offensive to the Seniors for whom she intended to read it. She was insulted, her husband accused me of jealousy, which was almost comical; her work was of a very low standard, and she was a woman in her late twenties, an air hostess in her early thirties who wore her hair in bunches on either side of her head like a bobby soxer. (American teen in the fifties)

And then the abuse fest started, so I left, in shock.

Divide and conquer – except it backfired badly. Most are now divorced. "Pigtails" and her boyfriend did a "midnight flit" and have not been heard from since as far as I know.

And the social worker divorced and remarried, and his family lost their older son, the marijuana addict, to Lou Gehrig's Disease.

RIP LS.

Another lost child of the Gulag.

XX

"ELMHURTS (sic) HOSPITAL

I had just filed incorporation papers with New York State for Petrani Inc. They contained plans for a small but select film company and for the manufacture of "portable" health foods, at that time very rare.

Today the supermarket shelves are stuffed with "natural" cookies, energy bars, etc. At that time, early eighties, there were only Tiger bars and a handful of others available in Health Food Stores. My foods were a step up, nutritionally, from those already on the market,at the time, but alas, I came down with another bout of double pneumonia – pleurisy; a consequence of the wretched schlepp-filled life on the Gulag. Up to that time it was difficult enough to get groceries, let alone obtain the rare and precious Homeopathic remedies that had previously catapulted my health from "chronic and recurring respiratory infections," to reasonable health. Without them, my health became critical and crashed under the duress and hell of life on the Alinsky Island Gulag.

 I was not the only one suffering from malnutrition due to the high prices and rotten food of the Catsimatides "patronage" supermarket. I did prevail on RIOC to supply a mini bus to Queens for the Seniors once a week, so they could afford food! However, I was not welcome. None of this is on record. I learned a sad secret on Crazy Island, and that is, in "America," if you want to accomplish something urgently, best let some mindless, unimaginative, ambitious bureaucrat take credit.

Valley Hospital, Ridgewood, NJ, had the best run Emergency Room in the Tri State area. After multiple episodes of abuse, incompetence, malpractice and such in the substandard hospitals serving Manhattan and the Isle of Woe, I felt that the distance required to go to Valley was more than compensated by the quality of care available there and the high level of competence and kindness of the staff.

This despite the fact that the cardiologist was a pill popping lecher who "tried it on" while I was attached to monitors and such. Fortunately the Hospital Chaplain stopped by and the creep ran. He died soon after, or so his colleague told me. In fact, John Strobeck, MD, is still in practice despite losing his license in at least three states.

He needed treatment. Was not the most incompetent MD on the planet.

After travelling to and from Valley Hospital with double pleuro-pneumonia, I slept well, but was alone and without food. No delivery service on crazy island, unless you wanted to live on pizza, from a pizzeria taken over by Mid Eastern owners and chili charging Mexican cooks Once the Italians left, after a lawsuit for calling their pizzeria "La Piccola Mela," which apparently violated the copyright of one of the denizens who had nicknamed the Gulag "The Little Apple," the chili sauce and spices started creeping into the marinara sauce.

It is now almost impossible to buy Marinara sauce without the ubiquitous chili oil. Wouldn't be surprised if sales have dropped significantly around the nation.

It was morning when the doorbell rang. I was feeling a little better but was still in my pyjamas as I made my way downstairs to the narrow, ridiculous, fire hazard of a "hallway" and opened the door.

A large solid object was smashed into the left side of my face. I fell backward and passed out. I have no idea for what duration. I woke up and was bleeding profusely from a wound just above my eye. The hallway was tiny, and in order to call 911, I would have to crawl back up the stairs. I was in shock and not thinking straight.

I opened the door and still in my robe walked mechanically to the Security Office. This was before I knew just how dangerous they had become. There were a couple of decent human beings there at the time, one was a black woman named Norma, who brought a gauze pad for my head, knelt down and wiped my blood soaked shoes against my objections; helped me back to my apartment to change my clothes while they called for an ambulance and then helped me into the ambulance. I was later able to save her job and very grateful to do so.

The EMTs were disgusting. The wound had not yet ecchymosed and swollen, but it was visible and my speech was slurred and broken. No half way intelligent person would mistake those symptoms for drunkenness.

They were telling me to hurry up. Repeating questions, not in a professional way, but in a hostile, "make fun of the stupid woman" way, and making derogatory remarks such as "call that an emergency." I don't know if the nasty Captain O'Loughlin who tried to drag my dying husband out of his bed one January 9, 1997, was in charge of the unit at the time, but it was certainly his style and lack of professionalism. He was also part of the gang that tried to abduct me from my apartment on Nov 2, 2006 with intent to homicide.

They scraped the bottom of the barrel when it came to services on or for Roosevelt Island!

I requested that a member of the NYPD accompany me in the ambulance, and one very kindly did. The NYPD was the only decent professional body connected with Main Street, but they were "handcuffed" to and limited by the domestic terrorists aka Roosevelt Island Public Safety – RIPS.

Arriving at Elmhurst I was met by a very nasty Resident and an intern. There was one other patient there, who was lying on a gurney and groaning. They and the nurses ridiculed him.

The nasty Resident had pin point pupils and said to the EMT "Call that an Emergency!" The EMTs sneered in my direction and left.

The previous night I had a confirmed diagnosis of double pneumonia-pleurisy from Valley Hospital, Ridgewood, New Jersey, the benchmark for ER Trauma services and a hospital of very high overall standards at the time. May still be a place of excellence.

The nasty Resident challenged Valley's diagnosis –"How do you know you have pneumonia! Who told you that you have pneumonia!" etc. He shut up when I told him my friend was the Director of the Trauma Unit there, then put on a butterfly bandage and said I had to stay to be examined by the Pulmonary Specialist. The equally nasty intern / male nurse, an ingratiating creep, that I call "Renfield Spiders," put me in a gurney and shoved me out into the hallway to wait for Dr Ceppenos.

I had brought a box of tissues from my apartment, and one of the nurses grabbed it out of my hand. It was clearly not hospital supply but she was spiteful. I told her it was mine and she had to return it. She didn't, but a young black adolescent, mopping the floor, waited till she left then brought me another box of tissues, hospital issue and not as soft, but most welcome and left quickly. I hope that God has blessed him for that singular act of compassion. Ghastly as it was for a few hours, the poor lad had to work there at least five days a week, probably for peanuts.

During all this I was extremely weak, shocked and disoriented. I could not breathe without pain, and there was no public transport to the Gulag. Someone gave me $5.00 for a taxi. I was also extremely anaemic and had not had any food for about 14 hours.

Ceppenos came down. He was a short, nasty, Hispanic peasant. No breeding, no manners, no intelligence, just a piece of paper with "MD" written on it and God alone knows how he acquired that.

Without any examination he started with the "You don't have pneumonia!" "You don't have a fever!" I replied that I'd been on antibiotics from the previous night – superior Homeopathic remedies not being available. After a little more wrangling he called over the nasty tissue thief nurse and said "Get her out of here…"

At that point a Hospital Administrator came down, a black woman named "Aisha Mohammed." She asked how Ceppenos had behaved and I told her. She said that they "had a lot of trouble with him and could I write a complaint?" I said yes, too weak to add "…as soon as I recover from double pneumonia – pleurisy, and can breathe again, and this pain and swelling in my right temple diminishes."

As soon as she left the freaky ER doctor called the Security Guard and told him to get me out. He was a big black guy. Sorry now that I did not call the NYPD, but any person, *any person,* voluntarily going into a New York Hospital or Emergency Room alone is setting themselves up for abuse. They were perfectly capable of lying, sending the NYPD away and sticking me in a psyche ward. I, obviously did not look so great, having dressed in a hurry, and being pale, hypoxic and slightly disoriented, but there is no excuse whatsoever for that abuse.

I walked out, and spent the next hour holding onto the rails outside Elmhurst Hospital with the sun beating down on me, the ER nurse sneering from the doorway, and vulnerable to any predator, and Elmhurst, Queens, has no shortage of them.

Suddenly an English voice, gentle, kind, well bred, spoke quietly into my ear. "Are you alright? Can I help you?" An angel from the Isle of Wight – near my home ground of Hampshire – by the name of John Stein offered me his arm and assisted me into his boss's Bentley. He called a couple of times to assure himself of my well-being, but by the third call, I was "losing it."

I had a call for an ATT commercial the following day, by which time the "call this an emergency" trauma had blown into the size and appearance of a multi-hued potato. I still wanted to go, and wove my way onto the tram and down Third Avenue. Fortunately it was not too far from the tram.

Improvisation was once one of my more enjoyable skills, but "not today, Josephine." Concentrating on keeping the wounded side away from the camera, I could hear myself slipping and sliding, barely able to put two words together.

Professional sabotage at every end of the spectrum.

The Casting Director was very kind, offered to call a cab, but I wanted to feel free and walk. Again the sun was very bright and in my face, going up Third Avenue, exacerbating photophobia, which I had not anticipated. I started weaving again.

A School crossing guard attached to the High School of Design off 57th Street, offered assistance and found a kindly lady to walk me back to the tram.

There are some decent people in NY. Most of them are in hiding, or return to the suburbs after dark.

On the third day I tried again to get help. I could feel the gears slipping, thoughts not connecting, my eidetic memory fading and the protrusion around my eye was massive – multicolored "tennis ball." I took the shuttle bus to New York Hospital where a Resident with a modified "shiner" put on a butterfly bandage, took no X-Rays and told me he got his black eye playing basketball and mine would get better soon too.

SNAP!

NOT!

Mine was deeper, far more severe, and inflicted on a person already severely hypoxic and without any family or social support whatsoever. No victim's assistance, NADA, NADA, NADA. He was well nourished, no apparent respiratory afflictions, good skin colour and tone, suggesting adequate oxygenation, therefore strong probability of a normal, healthy, rapid recovery. Logic and objective analysis appear to have fled America's Medical schools, leaving MDs to resort to psychology and psychologists to practice medicine, and too often, the sadists outnumber the "saints."

For the next two years on Looney Toons Island, I was "prey." I am not sure to this day whether it was the injury, exacerbated by my hypoxic condition or the sheer level of relentless abuse and emotional trauma at that wretched excuse for a hospital. How DARE they claim to treat illness or injury, when they take every opportunity to

ABUSE any patient unaccompanied by a protective or influential loved one.

Ironically, after my experiences with the maternity division of Lenox Hill Hospital I made it a point to accompany anyone who needed support. *No one should ever enter a NY Hospital unaccompanied by friend or family.*

I never did write the letter about Elmhurst. Three days later everything shut down and the next two years are a blur…my poor children had to cope for themselves and became prey to the vultures on Loony Toons Island.

Re Astoria General: AG is another Hospital run by the multi-cultural utopia of the Borough of Queens. With 171 languages, or thereabouts, along with a multitude of different cultural codes and standards, communications fail and the general population falls prey.

An Italian friend, "Nina," invited me to dinner with her friends for a girl's night out. These included a "barefoot" Greek peasant woman, "Medusa," married to a "barefoot" Greek peasant man, "Ari," who made it to medical school, supposedly to help his peasant people, but instead came to the USA. Greek peasant brought hubbie "Ari" along. He was a bit green about the gills, somewhat inebriated and started picking on my English accent, and how we stole Cyprus or something, Nina's husband – another doctor – was not invited, but sat in the living room looking daggers at Nina, in the hope that she'd stop "Ari's" drunken abuse.

To no avail, but suddenly he stopped and appeared stone cold sober. He told me he had opened up a kid to remove the gall bladder, found the gall bladder to be perfectly sound and healthy, but removed it anyway and threw it in the medical waste can. Nice one, "Ari."

That was about par for Astoria General. I was once brought there with no pulse, no BP, and left to lie on a gurney for two hours after which I realised it was getting dark and I would be safer at home. I walked out into a taxi! The brief whiffs of oxygen in the ambo worked. Humid low oxygen NY summer.

In the meantime, NY Hospital failed for thirty years to diagnose a condition I had correctly diagnoses at the age of 12.

IDIOTS.

New York is no place to be sick. Definitely not a place to die.

The Surrogates Court will try to steal your gravesite, declare you an indigent, and dump you in Potters Field for removal in a Chinese freighter to Europe.

In other words, New York City and State are so bankrupt they have taken to SELLING BODIES.

My friend, Thomas James Henry has three death certificates – the original, the fake for the City and the third, final and correct one.

Because they tried to steal his gravesite and sell his body after Memorial Sloan Kettering had finished with him and dumped him out. As they do when they have milked every last gram of insurance and Medicaid from a sick and dying patient.

They thought he was alone, but I fought for him. Again, gratitude to the honest Medical Examiner from England!

To the best of my knowledge Tom is buried in a beautiful Catholic cemetery run by the Archdiocese of New York.

He was my "buddyguard" on the Gulag, and witness to many of the horrors and violations there including the attempted murder and such.

RIP, Tom and Thank you.

Fred von Stange, Director of the USIS, Film and TV department, also knew something was terribly wrong there. He occasionally provided the courtesy of a drive home in his beloved Lincoln Sedan. This was always a blessed relief from the Tram or the subway train to hell.

He did his best to help us get out of there, even bringing a senior military officer from DC to meet me.

But that was the week of the assault when I was still stunned and in shock. He gave me his card and number and in my traumatised state I lost it.

Fred retired soon after and died two years later, possibly from accumulative toxicity related to the epoxies used to adhere the vinyl sidings to his house.

If so, it wasn't worth it.

For the record, there was no affair, no impropriety.

He was an officer and a true gentleman. Needless to say, a Republican.

XXI

CHURCH AND STATE AND COLUMBIA U AGAIN

Fr Benedict Groeschel was the Spiritual Director of the Archdiocese of New York. He had a Doctorate in Education degree with a specialty in psychology from Columbia University, taught at a college not eight miles from Langley, and considerable influence in the assignment of clergy.

As the therapist for many clergy, he had a vested interest in seeing them do well. Did he know how crazy the Island was, or did he genuinely believe it was a "nice, quiet, safe" place to assign priests who had experienced difficulties in their previous postings?

As an alumnus of the notorious Columbia U, home to the Frankfurt School of Marxism, and student of or participant in *psychology, i.e., the mind control experiments used to "entertain" contemporary students*, his connection with Roosevelt Island makes absolute, if sinister sense. He had to know of it, about it, and have some academic interest in it.

I'd prefer to think that his perception was off rather than his integrity and ethics were skewed. After all, who in their right mind could imagine the lunacy of life on Isle of Woe!

Wikipedia's selective account of the Gulag makes it appear interesting, historical, reasonably sane, even for New York, but it was insanity on steroids.

In his later years, Fr Benedict created great controversy by imputing seduction by a child or young teenager as a causal factor in sexual abuse cases and in mitigating a Child Rapist's culpability by suggesting that a man "*having a nervous breakdown" would not be able to <u>resist</u> a child.* Next question – why would a man in such a state, id est, who had lost control of his mental faculties, have access to a child?

In a National Catholic Register interview published August 27th, 2012, Fr Groeschel suggested that *"a minor is "the seducer" in "a lot" of sexual abuse cases. He said he was inclined to think that abusers on their first offense should not go to jail "because their intention was not committing a crime."*

Seriously? Did he not recognise the PATHOLOGY???? He was a *psychologist!* What does that tell us about the rest of them! Was he that naïve – or arrogant – Or deep down, a "Blame the Victim" Liberal?

This was the Spiritual Director of the Archdiocese of New York, appointed by the reputedly homosexual, Cardinal Cooke and maintained by the eminent John, Cardinal O'Connor, a kindly priest from Pennsylvania.

While that statement was made after Fr Groeschel's car accident, it does suggest that Fr Groeschel's insight into the human psyche was more Freud than St. Francis!

It was not the only questionable judgment on Fr Groeschel's part.

Was Fr Groeschel part of the "Great Design" of the NWO?

Did he consult with Columbia U School of Sociology on the planning of the Island? Did he have a role to play in the selection of the clergy assigned there? For each pastor, it was their first assignment as parish priest, and each pastor was a "first timer" with "baggage."

There was one Church to be shared by all denominations as well as being used as a Community Centre and meeting place for the dictators at RIOC. That would have to be by agreement with the Archdiocese. It was initially also used as a synagogue and mosque

A multi-culti community would have to include Catholics – the more liberal, however, the better, apparently but no provision was made for our *Sacramental* Offices.

The Sacred and Profane do not mix.

The Jews left, found their own place of prayer, and the moslems too, leaving the Protestant and Catholic clergy in an uneasy alliance.

Oliver Chapin didn't like Catholics. He accused us – yawn – of "praying to statues." I asked "why, if (he) didn't like statues and memorials, did he place a plaque to his mother inside the Church?" I liked Chapin – there was a plain spoke honesty about him and he was able to put aside his prejudices to hire me as the Protestant chapel organist.

This opened the door to a whole different world from the suffocating Island "Main Street," and led the way to a fortuitous meeting with Dr John Vecchione, Medical Director of Goldwater Hospital, the sister Hospital to Coler, and some historical work there.

I am the first Homeopath in a century to consult in an NY Hospital on ICU, MRSA, Post Thrombosis and Chronic care. Thank you and RIP Rev Oliver.

I was never *invited* to participate in *anything* at Cabrini Parish, unless, as the notorious Fr Peter Miqueli put it, they were "desperate!"

The first RC pastor had never run a parish. He was in charge of the cemetery in Staten Island and would not allow grieving parents to put both a cross and a headstone on the graves of their young sons who returned from 'Nam in a body bag. It was "either, or!" He would have come to Fr Benedict's attention when the Italian Nonnas took out a full page ad opposing him. Don't mess with grieving Italian grandmas!

Still, Fr McCarthy was conservative, orthodox, true to his calling. Yes, he did have a difficult personality but could be otherwise delightful. He was a lovely man in many ways, but hardly a match for the liberal multi-culti tower of babel hodgepodge that was the island's "tolerant" utopia.

He was followed by the liberal's dream, Fr Gorman, doing his doctorate in "Ministry" at NY Theological Seminary, a Protestant School, and full of the joys of liberation theology, Fr Matthew Fox and the notorious witch Starhawk, an associate of the current Irish "Minister for (killing) Children," American witch, Katherine Zappone To complete his doctorate Fr Gorman organised parish committees. I was on the drugs and alcoholism one and, with the consent of all, invited Lt Lisi, Commander of the NYPD Narcotics Division to give a talk. The good man agreed, but the night before his talk, the "Committee" abruptly cancelled it.

Not very smart of the coke-heads. Lisi set up a task force, caught a major source of cocaine dealing out of Soros' fave café, and closed them down!

A priest may go astray or try to flee the exigencies of a true calling, but unless he has completely gone over to the dark side, the ontological effects of ordination protect a certain sweetness and nobility of character.

Despite all his efforts, that of the leftward parishioners and the feminist nun assigned to assist him, and to whom he assigned much of his pastoral authority, Fr Gorman couldn't escape the innate kindness of his nature and sacerdotal calling.

Gorman was certainly well acquainted with Fr Benedict, acquainted enough to bring him to the Gulag along with the six other founders of the Franciscans of the Renewal.

Retrospectively I wonder how much Fr Benedict knew or understood about the Gulag. As a doctoral alumnus of Columbia U he must have encountered feedback or "scatter" regarding the experimental new community

Was he part of the decision to "unify" the churches under one roof?

Fr Benedict's doctorate was in Education, with a speciality in psychology from *Columbia University.* I don't know much about Columbia U, other than abortion/child rape advocate Ruth Bader Ginsberg is a graduate; Obama has history there, apparently covered up by Columbia U, and I am definitely prejudiced after the plagiarist Professor of Drama there, Isaiah Sheffer, stole my Joyce / Bloomsday Festival. The plan for the Gulag came from the Columbia U School of Sociology, which is linked to their Psych department as well as to the Frankfurt School of Marxism, and the "usual suspects."

Fr Benedict also was an adjunct professor at the ominously named "Institute for Psychological Sciences" in *Arlington, Virginia,* which is close to DC, and eight miles from Langley Virginia, headquarters of the CIA. Nothing sinister or MK Ultra there!

The "Institute for Psychological Science" is a "Catholic academy," where Fr Benedict taught an annual intensive course focused on providing "practical assistance to people experiencing trauma, extreme stress and sorrow, i.e., *extremely vulnerable*, while at the same time integrating religious values into counselling and psychotherapy."

He was also the pastoral psychologist at St Joseph's Seminary, Dunwoodie, the Spiritual Director of the Archdiocese of NY, the founder of the Trinity Retreat and co-founder, with seven other Capuchins, of the Community of Franciscans of the Renewal. Whatever he knew, and however involved he may have been, bringing the six other founders of the Renewal to the Gulag was a transformational blessing. The six other founders were: Fr Pio Mandato, (Now FMHJ) Fr Glen Sudano, Br/Fr Bob Stannion, RIP, Br/Fr Bob Lombardo, Br. Lawrence, and Br/Fr Stan Fortuna.

Perhaps he was over-extended, but he did have an "army" of educated young men at his beck and call while he wrote his books. I admit to "wishful thinking" as I edit my pages *toute seule!*

Three of the original founders eventually left, one of whom was described as the "real fire in the community." He always took a discreet and humble role, yet somehow managed to steal Benedict's thunder.

Even on that crazy Island with its Liberation Theology pastor and Feminasty "nice safe abortions" nun, people instinctively flocked to Fr Pio, the "fire," hungry for the word, hungry for the Truth.

The CFRs gave a retreat on the Gulag, concluding with the Sacrament of Reconciliation. I believe it started about 7 pm. Only one person, a nurse, went to the Lib Theology pastor, Fr Gorman – because she "felt sorry for him," but people were lining up for Fr Pio after 11pm, even as the central heating went off and the church became very chilly.

That, in a place, where spiritual awareness was confused, and often dark, the Light shone and overcame the darkness.

There is more to say, but why and how did Fr Benedict obtain such control over the Archdiocese of NY, the Seminary, the CFRs and the crazy Gulag? Was he fast tracked by his connections at the Columbia-Frankfurt School of Marxism? Or the little school near Langley, Virginia, home of the CIA?

If he was so inspired and erudite, why didn't he see the aberrations at Dunwoodie, aberrations that led to a decadent homosexual cartel gaining great power and influence in the USA and Rome? Why didn't he recognise a certain choir director as a fraud and predator – who became the Director of Priests' Personnel and protector of now notorious Fr Peter Miqueli, pastor on the Gulag, for twelve whole years? Back to him later.

Why was Fr Gorman, a gentle but troubled priest, appointed as pastor to such a complex and challenging parish? He had never run a parish before, was recovering from a severe accident, took a degree in theology from a protestant seminary, and promoted liberation theology. He almost immediately abdicated his role to Sister Regina who came to Isle of Woe after two years recovering from depression elsewhere and called herself the "Associate Pastor."

She appointed pro-abortion Sandra Neis as Eucharistic Minister and allowed distribution of Communion to persons of all faiths. Sandra was a black feminist ambitious to enter politics. With her inseparable companion, a married teacher of the disabled, M, as campaign manager, she schmoozed her way to the Presidency of the PTA, using it as a stepping stone to the City Council. In order to qualify as a candidate for City Council, she had to collect a certain number of signatures, which she did by going to the Hospitals North and South of the Gulag and obtaining names and signatures from patients, some of whom did not speak English, others of whom were *non compos mentis.*

Talk about exploitation!

Regina and her twin sister, also a Cabrini nun, were child actors / extras in Hollywood – which may have influenced her concept of religious life… She ran the thrift shop, and at one of their annual "Fashion Shows," dressed in robes as the "Reverend Reggie" and "officiated" at a fake wedding ceremony – oblivious to the impropriety and optics of a 28year old man with a 15 year old bride! Previously, Regina taught kindergarten, *oy vae*!

Fr Gorman saw no impropriety. I have seen other priests misguided by ambitious, possessive women, jealous of their status. Tragic.

At one point, observing me returning one of Fr Gorman's Lib Theology books, with challenges to the content, she moved closer to him and announced that she "undresses in front of the window because if anyone sees me they deserve what they get…"

Fr Gorman turned bright red – there was an innocence to him – and henceforth followed her like a sick puppy. He later announced to the congregation that she was his "factotum – which as you men know, is another name for *wife…*"

She made sure to exclude me from Parish functions.

Years later a mutual love of Chesterton triggered a psychotic break in yet another female Church worker in WA State who kidnapped my grandson in an apparent jealous rage over her "factotum," a gentle, erudite, and innocent, Polish priest, Fr M, RIP. He was quickly transferred by Archbishop Sartain, with no concern or consideration for the trauma to our family by the unbalanced Church employee.

Dear Fr A: "You're saying that the love of Chesterton made Father M holy?

Me: (silently) "No, I'm saying it made him *dead!*" But that's for another book.

Note to self: do not discuss books or theology with clergy in the presence of jealous, possessive, power hungry or inappropriately inquisitive female Church employees...

I don't know if anyone saw a conflict of interest between one man, Fr Benedict, controlling the hearts and minds of the troubled clergy and religious, both in the seminary and in the assignment of parishes, as well as co-founding a religious order and being Spiritual Director of the Archdiocese.

It is just too weird or coincidental that the blue-print for Roosevelt Island was designed by Columbia U aka the Frankfurt School of Marxism / Columbia School of Sociology; that Fr Benedict Groeschel who received his doctorate from U Columbia Dept of Education but with a specialty in psychology, would send his "successes," i.e. priests he had counselled, albeit inexperienced in parish administration and with baggage, to Roosevelt Island, or that he had even heard of it when most citizens of the USA were oblivious to its existence.

Psychology is the "servant" or covert wing of Freud-Marx driven Sociology.

For a Franciscan Fr Benedict had sophisticated tastes; his hobbies were astronomy – for aspirants a kind of intellectual chic requiring expensive telescopes. He recounted that, every year, at Christmas, he would look in the mirror, raise a glass of Benedictine and say "here's to you, Benedict."

Years later, he was in a motor accident and sustained serious injuries, including a TBI. I doubt if anyone looked at *him* or treated him as if he were a specimen.

He had an army of young men to care for him, who will probably promote him for canonisation.

Columbia U will defo claim him then!

XXII

WRITING STRAIGHT WITH CROOKED LINES

Der Luft, der Wasser wie da Erde – Goethe

"From Water, Earth and Air unfolding

A thousand germs break forth and grow

In dry and wet and warm and chills

And had I not the Flame reserved, why really –

There's nothing special of my own to show..."

Goethe's Mephistopheles.

Goethe's "Sa*an" cannot create. Has nothing, but "dibs" on Fire.

Like certain aforementioned parties, the evil one can only purloin, plagiarize and steal – but yes, has reserved the flame; the fires are reserved not to forge and create, but to wound and to destroy, and even, they are not his Creation.

"*There's nothing special of their own to show...*

Fr Benedict did offer this quotation: "God writes straight with crooked lines." He said it was Hispanic. It means that God can and does bring Good out of evil.

God always has "*something special of His own to show!*" It is all "His" to start with!

When Fr Gorman came to the Island, the butterfly bandage was still on my brow.

It was not long thereafter that Fr B and the other founders of the Community of Franciscans of the Renewal came to the Gulag. I was still feeling the effects of the assault, too frightened to say anything about the keys in the freezer or the broccoli in the cutlery drawer, in case I was accused of misdiagnosed by yet another misogynist - especially after the abuse at "Elmhurts." One doctor and a Cabrini nun, President of the Cabrini Hospital Board once insisted that I "wanted to be ill."

The nun never changed but the doctor's expression when he finally took an X-Ray and found DOUBLE PNEUMONIA was priceless. He turned almost as white as the neon backlight on the X-Ray monitor!

I have been misdiagnosed by almost every MD that I ever encountered, including a few "Professors" of Medicine. I was not about to risk that. It was lonely. There was no one in my corner. For the record, I made the correct diagnoses when I was 12.

In the sick and Draconian world of the "liberal" i.e., *totalitarian* Democrat, any reason sufficed to remove a child from his/her mother, particularly when the mother in question was pro Life and Conservative.

On that vicious Island, "RF" was trying her utmost to get rid of me, and I was afraid of a politically influenced quick and superficial diagnoses made by the incompetents in New York's Hospitals, and that I would not be able to raise my children, if I showed any weakness or made any complaint.

And then came the "great" Fr Benedict who treated me as if I were a specimen, and complimented me on having a name that means "woman of sorrows."

I needed help. I was in shock after the abuses experienced on the Gulag and was hoping that this new Franciscan reform order would help, and they did.

At least Fr Pio did.

Most of the Founders of the Franciscans of the Renewal were really great – each unique and talented. Brother Bob, later ordained *Fr* Robert Stannion was warm and kindly, knew every herb, rare or common; Fr Glenn, gentle and kindly, more reserved; Brother Larry, a gifted carpenter, insightful and down to earth; Brother Stan, now Fr Stan, a gifted musician, and Fr Pio, wow! I'll put it this way – that despite Fr Benedict's "bells and whistles" all flocked to the humble, unassuming Fr Pio.

A friend, Mary Ann Sullivan, special Ed teacher at Coler Hospital, and aka "The Vatican Spy" knew the biographies of every priest in the Archdiocese of NY backwards, forwards and standing on her head, including the hierarchies! For her "files," she asked (then) Brother Bob who was really in charge, i.e., who was the leader of the CFRs. Without hesitation, Brother Bob said "Benedict is our Superior," but indicating Fr Pio, quietly setting the altar, he added decisively, "but *he* is the FIRE in the Community."

Brother (Fr) Bob was very curious about the Island. He said was immediately reminded of the town which St Francis exorcised. He had the spiritual discernment of a holy man.

It can't have been easy for Fr Benedict, with all his influence and intra Catholic celebrity and socialite sponsors, to know that the wounded heart of humanity always turned to the humble, kindly, perceptive, priest born in Pietrelcino, Italy – Fr Pio Mandato.

He was my lifesaver in that Gulag. It was as if a rescue helicopter had arrived and scooped me out of a burning lake or savage sea and I was devastated when he and eleven or twelve other men left the CFRs to form another Community in faraway Massachusetts, so devastated that I actually took driving lessons passed my test and got on the road!

Some of those men were not sound, and had Fr Pio had not drawn them away from the main house, they would have made life very difficult for the new CFR Community.

He took the trouble makers with him and then was called to a strict eremitical life far from the "maddening" (sic) crowd for himself. When he left, other "good guys" left and joined other Franciscan Communities.

Thanks to a subsequent article on the Central Park jogger, I recognised the symptoms of Traumatic Brain Injury and was able to acquire the appropriate Homeopathic remedies to start the healing process – or continue the healing process started by Fr. Pio.

Word recall was difficult: from being the nine year old with the vocabulary and linguistic skills of an Oxford or Cambridge graduate, I had to stimulate word recall starting with the very simple crosswords in the Daily News, eventually working my way back up to the Sunday Times (UK) cryptics erstwhile in the NY Post and English Codewords.

Between the Homeopathic protocols and my mental agility exercises I had recovered everything except my trust in humanity, Fr Pio being the first exception.

Post script: Due to that assault, Petrani Inc. folded before its registration was finalised, but the plan and concepts described in the incorporation papers filed with NY State are making millions for others across the USA.

As did my Bloomsday Celebration and my rare and then arcane knowledge of the extraordinary healing protocol known as Homeopathic Medicine, currently being distorted for profit at the expense of humanity.

No doubt through the prayerful intercessions of persons mentioned here, I found a tiny candle in the darkness which led to the Hospital Chaplaincies and thence the opportunity to be the first Homeopath in a century to consult in a NY Hospital, on extremely serious conditions.

Thank you, Fr Pio.

Whatever, the Columbia connections of Fr Benedict, his favourite aphorism "God writes straight with crooked lines" proved true. The gates of Columbia's hell did not prevail, and a funny anti-Catholic Four Square Gospel Minister opened the door that *Fr Pio unlocked* and all worked to liberate a dear Copt Bishop, and, imo, saint, who had lain in the same hospital room for 18 months on a ventilator, tube fed, paralysed on one side, and subjected to antibiotic resistant infections, criticism and abuse, with no relief and abundant noise from the boom boxes of the other patients.

Does "God write straight with crooked lines," or do we just see the underside of God's exquisite embroidery.

I do know this - that, like myself, Monsignor also prayed for liberation from his surroundings, and our prayers were heard and answered.

While he never left the hospital, he spent his last years in an airy, private room, surrounded by books and affectionate visitors, providing a welcome support for the kindly Chaplain, Fr Tim Healy, SJ, and wheeling himself about the corridors, blessing his friends with a hand that they said "would never move again."

(For the record, by improving Msgr's health status to such a level that he could be moved from the Respiratory Unit to the Nursing Home Section, Homeopathy saved the State of New York over $3,000,000 over a 3 year period.

I will add here, that they will give credit to the Dobell diaphragmatic pace-maker, which they inserted against my recommendation. Monsignor's brother, a Director of Medicine at a Falls River Hospital, persuaded him that it was his duty as a priest to subject himself to medical experimentation. Yes, the patients in NY City Hospitals were experimental fodder.

Msgr was told, that irrespective of the progress that he had made, they would not let him out without it and so he consented. 18 months on your back in the same room as three to five other people, most of whom come with boom boxes and animated relatives could make a contemplative like Monsigner pretty desperate.

I knew then that he would never leave the hospital and return to his Community, but was able to restore sufficient strength and stamina to allow him a day trip to N Jersey and several Papal Masses.

Hispanics seldom abandoned their families, and usually brought home cooked food, bless them, but they are prone to "boom boxes" – a nightmare to refined minds.

After all he had suffered and endured, now that a Homeopath had brought him to a previously unimagineable state of wellness, and near independence, they subjected him to yet another painful and agonising procedure.

After the procedure, I had to work hard again, to restore his physical health and functions to the point where we were able to take him out to the Papal Masses in Brooklyn and Central Park.

I came once and found that he had been put in isolation. His eyes were "red" so they decided he had MRSA! Hello! There was no mucus, no fever, no restlessness or any other indication of a STAPH infection!!!

Another time he went into a coma but I was able to place the correct Homeopathic remedy sub lingua, and a few hours later he awoke.

I called on Dr Vecchione who had been promoted to Medical Director and was not directly involved in Monsignors misdiagnosis, and he demanded tests and "liberated" poor Monsignor from Isolation.

Why were his eyes red? He had received word that his brother, the doctor from Fall River, had died. Too bad his brother didn't have a Homeopath too! After all, he had consented to my work.

Interestingly, Monsignor had studied in Lyons, France, home of Boiron, the Homeopathic Pharmacists. No "coincidences" in God's world!

With the hand that was "permanently" paralysed, Monsignor wrote a "Thank You" note to me. It is one of my most precious possessions, along with a "Thank You" note from St Mother Teresa.

I had the satisfaction of seeing him enjoy his final years, in a room filled with the books that he loved; and wheeling himself about the hospital, loving and loved by all he encountered.

While we were burying my late husband in Ireland, he was diagnosed with a bleeding ulcer – and bumped in an ambulance across the river to Bellevue. They gave him a transfusion and bumped him back to Goldwater where he went into a second coma. This time I did not have the authority to treat him, so I read Thomas Aquinas in Latin to him, and he always responded in some way. Enjoy the Celestial Banquet, my friend!

XXIII

DA CAPO (Recap) – Corrupt to the core.

The sod was turned by Nelson Rockefeller, shortly before he died *in flagrante delicto* with his mistress.

He was NY's chief RINO - the Rockefellers, like their Rothschild cousins, play both sides of the political fence.

Speaking of Rothschild, the initial landscaper was a Rothschild associate, now all but vanished from the web.

The early residents were issued a *huge book length questionnaire.* I did not fill it in. Perhaps my refusal to co-operate with such an intrusive, unexplained invasion of my privacy along with our glowing reference from Ambassador Curley put us on the watch list, made us a target.

Or perhaps just the racial hatred and personal bitterness of the "Enforcer" along with her Rat Party connections was sufficient to damn us from the beginning.

The only way the "Enforcer" could have known that we were friends with a senior member of the NY GOP would be by unauthorised, ex officio access to our Housing Records.

The *questionnaire* is significant. Three decades later, Columbia U "students" showed up to check the results of their "experiment," just as hundreds of families were being forcibly evicted from their apartments, Gestapo style.

The Frankfurt School of Marxism was founded in Germany but found a "happy home" at Columbia University in NYC in 1934. Its purpose was to discourage the personal independent and enterprise beloved of Americans and create a cultural, financial, and psychological dependence on the State, i.e., full control by, and compliance with the "Nanny" State. America was to turn Communist by stealth and subversion rather than by the bullet and sword.

Using the clichéd but effective concepts of "divide and conquer," the Frankfurt School took the "usual suspects" i.e., malcontented minorities – blacks, women, homosexuals – and reinforced any nascent sense of victimhood. "Workers of the world unite – you've nothing to lose but your chains" became "victims of the world unite – you've everything to gain when we've subjugated the bright, independent, "get on with it," chin up, "fighting spirit," noble European Christians."

There are those like G. Edward Griffin of Freedom Force International who believe that Columbia U School of Sociology, aka The Frankfurt School of Marxism, NY HQ, has won.

I disagree.

The Gulag 10044 was, in no doubt, whatsoever, all theirs. But they did not achieve what they had hoped and expected.

The American Spirit was too strong.

America fought back.

America fought back and won the war.

America won because American liberty, free enterprise, tradition and foundational law, i.e., the US Constitution, allowed a young New York boy, born of European stock, and raised on the principles of the Founding Fathers: Liberty, Equality, Free Speech, the Right to Bear Arms, walk to the ramparts, hold up his fist and say "MAKE AMERICA GREAT AGAIN!!"

And we did.

Evil will still attack, but evil will not prevail.

Evil was able to turf out 600 or more families at the end of the Gulag experiment for which no one signed a contract.

Evil was able to harass innocent people, destroy children, their hopes, dreams, ambitions, careers, interest in life, their innocent joy.

Evil was able to drive women into nervous breakdowns, to take medications, where before their lives were relatively serene.

Evil was able to corrupt the Housing Court system in New York so that the eviction notices were issued and communities scattered around the five boroughs, the tri state area, and even the continental USA.

Evil was able to destroy careers, slander the just, steal from the charitable.

Evil was not able to bring its baby butchery abattoir onto that Island.

To escape evil I engaged in Hospital Ministry and thereby was called to consult as a Homeopath, on a man that had suffered intolerably for 18 months following a stroke.

He was hemiplegic, his right side completely paralysed; his infections from the "stoma" or feeding tube did not respond to the strongest antibiotics; some of the hospital staff ridiculed him if he groaned. He was a priest, he should not complain, they said, mockingly, like the low lifes mocking Christ on the cross.

Under my care and with the consent of a wonderful, dedicated, Italian trained physician, Dr John Vecchione, MD, he was soon free of infection, wheeling himself about the hospital, blessing patients and staff alike, and concelebrating Mass.

I could never get him out completely out of the hospital, thanks to a nurse in his community, who had the last word on leaving him there - but we had a delightful time at the Papal Masses in Brooklyn and Central Park.

The Hospital Ministry came out of an encounter with the Rev Chapin.

Wikipedia does not mention the Rothschild landscapers who created the "no private zones," the Clockwork Orange, 1984 effect. CCTV cameras were ubiquitous – until needed to prove malfeasance by Public Safety or an assassin set up by the local "Enforcer."

Back to the Church. Alinsky rules applied here two. The first Protestant Minister, Chaplain Chapin, kind of Dickensian in appearance, was forced to move from the perfectly sound Hospital Residence to the smaller, less sturdy fire traps designed by award winning designer, Philip Johnson. As no dogs were allowed on the island he was forced to give up his dog.

He shot it in Main Street in protest, or so I was advised by an "eye witness."

Before I knew about the dog, I liked him. He wasn't fond of Catholics, but I knew where I stood with him. He was honest, even forthright and, kind enough, despite the dog incident. He had been a missionary in Africa. I suppose that is where he learned to shoot, as he, also, was a liberal. Under the skin of every liberal beats a heart of anger.

Under the guise of commiserating with the patients of Coler Hospital for their hospital diet – which was surprisingly good for such a large institution, if heavy on the collard greens – Chapin would describe his own misery – growing up in the recession days, when his father was a minister and the people had no money for the collection.

He was Four Square Gospel by training and inclination, but also served the Episcopalians and Presbyterians and Methodists.

He told the patients sitting quietly in their wheel chairs that people receive care packages, and they would share their food with his family because they had no money.

And then came the clincher…"the only food they shared was oatmeal. All they ever received was oatmeal…!"

Even in his sixties, the angry little boy came out – oatmeal, always oatmeal! Like the Israelis in the desert – "Quail again, Moses?!"

Between his hospital salaries and his income from the Protestant Parish, he would never have to eat oatmeal again – or even look at it!

But the memory lingered…and the Alinskyites forced him to give up his dog when they shut down the perfectly sound 700 apartment "Nurses Residence" and dispersed the staff of Goldwater–Coler around the three boroughs.

Having no place to put the faithful German Shepherd, he brought it to the Church plaza and publicly shot it in testimony against them.

I was not a witness to this, just heard it recounted by persons who claimed to have witnessed it themselves.

It's curious that God used an anti-Catholic Protestant Minister, a Jesuit Mathematician turned Chaplain, the Conservative Catholic daughter of a far left Irish politician, and even the Columbia U Sociologist-Priest as the instrument for significant relief from suffering for a Latin and Coptic Rite Hieronymous or Bishop, an American MD trained in Italy – all linked together by the prayers of a humble Italian Franciscan born in Pietrelcina.

So much Love in that. And intricacy.

But the Lord God, the Creator of Heaven and Earth, must have a whale of a sense of humour! Just look at that package! Peace and Good Will!

St Francis of Assisi calls the devils "God's policemen…" It appears that they are sometimes allowed to give us an unpleasant push to get us out of a rut and back on God's path again.

Must be so frustrating for the "bad guys" when the Lord always turns "all to the good."

Thanks be to God.

XXIV

Postlude.

TIMELINE TO "AUFHEBUNG DER KULTUR" i.e., CULTURAL ANNIHILATION.

FROM FREUD TO FRAUD

1890	Freud publishes "Civilisation and its Discontents."
	Frankfurt School of Marxism. Gramsci, Lukacz etc.
	Marx wanted war to trigger socialist revolution. Did this lead to collusion with the Ottomans. A Turk triggered WWI, Turkey colluded with Nazi Germany during WWII and later a Turk attempted to assassinate Pope John Paul II. (Ottoman, i.e., Islamic war against Europe for 600 years)
1910	Historic meeting on Jekyll Island established "The Federal Reserve," turning control of America's currency – and economy – back to the London-Frankfurt based imperialist banking system.
1913	Rothschilds allegedly blackmail Woodrow Wilson into signing the Federal Reserve Act. This gives them control of almost unlimited wealth with which to broker and wage wars – at high interest.

1914	Turk assassinated the Archduke of Austria. WWI begins
	Rothschilds allegedly fund Bolsheviks?
1915	Armenian Genocide by Turkey
1917	Assassination of Tsar Nicholas. Bolshevik Revolution, funded by Rots. Bolsheviks creep into the USA disguised as refugees. Infiltration and take-over of America's educational systems from kindergarten to college begins.
1918	End of WWI. Gramsci and Lukacz disappointed that the war united the "proletariat" instead of bringing global instability and revolution.
1918	Gramsci imprisoned. Dies in prison. Lukacz as Minister of Culture in Hungary developed concept of *cultural terrorism, i.e., derision and rejection of Christian values and ethics.* Hungarians reject this.
1919	Romania invades Hungary.
	Criticised vehemently for their role in WWI, the Rothschild's buy up Reuters, then AP, then create their own media empires – NBC – Rockefeller Center, Time Life, Newsweek, etc.
1923	Lukacz and Marxist Frank Weil meet in Frankfurt for a study. The term

"Political Correctness"[iv2] is born. Weil accepts Lukacz cultural assassination program.

Weil funds the Institute for Social Research aka Frankfurt School of Marxism. (FSM)

1929   JP Morgan – ex "Jekyll Island" dumps stock leading to the infamous Wall Street Crash shortly after Hoover's election as 31st President of the USA. Hoover was a humanitarian who spent most of his working life abroad and was not a DC "insider." He lasted one term.

1930   Max Horkheimer becomes director of Frankfurt School of Marxism. BRINGS IN SIGMUND FREUD!

"Workers" are not only oppressed by "masters," but *psychologically controlled by the "discontents" of Civilization!*

1933   FDR is elected President and plants the seeds of socialism in the USA,

1933   The grandson of an illegitimate alliance between a Rothschild millionaire and his maid, id est Adolph Schickelgruber Hitler, take over Germany. Nazis gain a foothold

---

[2] Wikipedia notes "In early to mid-20th Century, the phrase "politically correct" was associated with the dogmatic application of Stalinist doctrine, debated between Communist Party members and Socialists – all the way back to the Frankfurt School of Marxism…

in Europe. Does Nazi refer to National Socialist – or to AshkeNazi i.e. the Khazarian Tartars "adopted" by Jewish gold traders?

1934 FSM moves to Columbia U in New York, the cultural epicentre of the globalist world. (London was the economic epicentre – all foreign transactions passed through the Rothschild held City of London banks.

First paper published was "Critical Theory" – criticising everything the civilized world had previously cherished.

1939 Hitler and Stalin invade Poland simultaneously, knowing the courageous Poles would fight to the death for Christ and against the annihilation of the Christian world, and were thereby an "obstacle" to world dominion. Both Hitler and Stalin are allegedly funded by the Rothschilds. True or not, there's an awful lot of dense smoke billowing from that fire!

1941 Japan invades Pearl Harbor.

1945 Yalta. FDR hands Poland, Hungary, Bulgaria, Romania and the rest of Eastern Europe over to Stalin.

1949	After murdering 60 million Chinese, Mao Tse Tung establishes the "Peoples' Republic of China," i.e., Communist China where the people *have no control over their own lives.*

Vietnam, Afghanistan, Cambodia, Drug wars, Pakistan murders 4,000,000 Hindi in 1973, Iraq, Iran, WTC (9/11) Weaponised Social Divisions, Weaponised Social Media, Suppression of Free Speech, imposition of Forced Speech, LAWFARE...

GAME, SET AND MATCH TO THE COMMUNAZIS?

NOT SO FAST!

USA SAID NO!

USA MUST GO?

NO FLAMING WAY!

LINKS AND REFERENCES

Updates on "Loony Tunes Island," where the Residents are still telling themselves they have representation by electing a toothless Roosevelt Island Residents' Association, which betrayed and let down the residents for decades.

Roosevelt Island Public Safety is still up to its sleazy tricks as the following links will reveal. Joyce Short, formerly Joyce Maynard has recently filed a report with the Inspector General.

Many years ago, RIPS arrested Joyce Maynard for removing discarded bricks from a dumpster for her garden. RIPS called the NYPD who told them, more or less, to get lost and stop wasting the taxpayers' time and money. I liked her, she is honest and forthright, like Lisa K, also harassed and threatened by RIPS. Apparently, she is still there and fighting, in the belief that the Gulag operates under the Constitution of the USA and American Law.

http://rooseveltislander.blogspot.com/2018/02/roosevelt-island-residents-rally-last.html

https://nypost.com/2013/06/16/roosevelt-island-security-chief-quits-amid-lawsuits-alleging-officer-brutality/

http://www.nypress.com/some-island-residents-say-that-local-public-safety-officers-arent-held-accountable-for-their-actions/

http://www.ny1.com/nyc/all-boroughs/news/2018/02/28/public-pressure-from-residents-of-roosevelt-island-yields-a-long-awaited-arrest-for-lewd-behavior

https://web.archive.org/web/20150704024141/http://www.dnainfo.com/new-york/20120503/roosevelt-island/tech-campus-leaves-hospital-patients-worried-about-future#

http://kallosforcouncil.com/share/roosevelt-island-public-safety-stories - one of these accounts includes Cesar aka Wilson Toro, a RIPS thug, registered sex offender and one of the freaks that made the attempt on my life in collusion with two rogue EMTs, Ruger and Fellaria.

The crimes, felonies and Human Rights violations on the Gulag have been ongoing for decades now, and nothing, it appears, has changed.

Rene Bryant should have put me up for a Crimestoppers award for identifying a dangerous cab driver wanted for assaulting a police officer. I wonder if a "relative" received that award instead. Same with the JTTF, whom I assisted in identifying a khat drugs funding terrorism ring, but after liaison with RIPS, JTTF tried to put me in extreme danger. Either they were incredibly stupid, or working with RIPS-Soros-RF to rid the world of the one person with their game plan at that time. The corruption just keeps spreading. Now RIPS "ossifers" are planted in PDs across the nation. Kind of explains the rash of abuses under Obama.

https://web.archive.org/web/20150704024141/http://www.dnainfo.com/new-york/20120503/roosevelt-island/tech-campus-leaves-hospital-patients-worried-about-future

This article claims that the relocation of Goldwater patients took place in 2012, and that four hundred patients were awaiting new homes. In fact thousands of patients were relocated upstate or in since 2006, if not sooner.

https://en.wikipedia.org/wiki/Columbia_University_protests_of_1968 Mark Rudd, former leader of the SDS, Students for a Democrat Society, who held CU faculty members hostage in protest against affiliation with IDA, i.e., Institute for Defense Analysis, was also connected with R Is. He moved his mother in law there! Lived in a large and beautiful apartment in Greenwich Village with skylights and a grand piano which no one could actually play. In fairness, before he cheated on his IRA sympathiser wife, she was, at least, trying to learn. His surprisingly sweet and mature daughter was an accomplished equestrienne. Horseback riding in Manhattan, grand pianos - funny thing about lefties - they're all wannabe aristocrats. Another associate of Holder-Obama.

https://en.wikipedia.org/wiki/Roosevelt_Island

Melville "was here" too. The son of the leader of the Attica riots and his mother were "founding members" of the Gulag. We "talked" after the first WTC bombing, and Josh seemed – initially - sympathetic to the bombers. He fulfilled his desire to be in show biz by becoming a porn producer in Florida.

https://en.wikipedia.org/wiki/Sam_Melville#Legacy

How it came to pass:

https://en.wikipedia.org/wiki/Yalta_Conference

Three men, Churchill, FDR, Stalin, carve up the world. Yep, three men distribute power and jurisdiction between UK, Soviets, USA but – on whose behalf?

1. Federal Reserve System, Jekyll island, History, Aldrich Plan, J ...

   www.jekyllislandhistory.com/federalreserve.shtml ... Jekyll island, History, Aldrich Plan, J. Pierpont Morgan, Historical, Dr. A. Piatt ... Through a non-stop flurry of meetings, he organized rescues of banks and trust ...

2. **How a secret meeting on Jekyll Island led to the Fed - Marketplace**
3. **https://www.marketplace.org/2015/10/20/economy/b ig-book/how-secret-meeting-jekyll-island-led-fed** Oct 20, 2015 ... The United States Federal Reserve has received a good deal of flack over the years. Whether it's ire over looming interest rate hikes or ...
4. Jekyll Island and the Creation of the Federal Reserve - YouTube

   https://www.youtube.com/watch?v=Xoz4jbEZzlc

   May 4, 2011 ... A clandestine meeting on Jekyll Island 100 years ago was a pivotal step ... of that historic meeting discusses the history of the Federal Reserve.

---

i

The Maginot Line was built by the French to keep Hitler's Germans out. On the Gulag, it served as a social divider, despite the "utopian" presentation of the Island.

1. ^{iv} **Political Correctness — A Rothschild Invention of Language ...**

humansarefree.com/2016/02/political-correctness-rothschild.html

"Nathan Rothschild had given Marx two checks for several thousand pounds to finance the cause of Socialism. The checks were put on display in the British Museum, after Lord Lionel Walter Rothschild, a trustee, had willed his museum and library to them." Both of these key New World Order families are thus implicated in Marxism, the Frankfurt School and political correctness.

2. **How Political Correctness of the Rothschild Frankfurt ...**

https://www.toolsforfreedom.com/product-p/1495.htm

Political correctness is a Rothschild invention. It comes from their think tank known as the Frankfurt school, which was set up in 1923 to work out how to spread collectivism (or its offshoots Socialism, Marxism and Communism) to the world. The real agenda of political correctness is to stifle objective investigation and free speech.

It is now being used by Facebook to "purge" Conservatives and pro Lifers from their Social Media network while allowing degrading, perverse, cruel and sexualized images to remain. Facebook is now referred to by many as "Fascistbook," "Farcebook" and other less polite terms beginning with "F." I have been suspended for an anti Nazi comment and a well-established historical reference. We are entering a world run by incognate robots.

3. Satan's Secret Agents: The Frankfurt School and their Evil ...

    https://www.darkmoon.me/2013/satans-secret-agents-the-frankfurt...

From "Need to Know News"

The 1950s were a simple, romantic, and golden time in America.

California beaches, suburbia, and style. *Atlas Shrugged* was published,

NASA was formed, and Elvis rocked the nation. Every year from 1950–

1959 saw over 4 million babies born. The nation stood atop the world in

every field.

It was an era of great economic prosperity in The Land of the Free.

Permission pending.

So, what happened to the American traits of confidence, pride, and

accountability?

The roots of Western cultural decay are very deep, having first sprouted

a century ago. It began with a loose clan of ideologues inside Europe's communist movement. Today, it is known as the Frankfurt School, and, through its NY home at Columbia U School of Sociology, its ideals have perverted American society.

<u>When Outcomes Fail, Just Change the Theory</u>

Before WWI, Marxist theory held that if war broke out in Europe, the working classes would rise up against the bourgeoisie and create a communist revolution.

Well, as is the case with much of Marxist theory, things didn't go too well. When war broke out in 1914, instead of starting a revolution, the proletariat put on their uniforms and went off to war.

After the war ended, Marxist theorists were left to ask, "What went wrong?"

Two very prominent Marxists thinkers of the day were Antonio Gramsci and Georg Lukács. Each man, on his own, concluded that the working class of Europe had been blinded by the success of Western democracy and capitalism. They reasoned that until both had been destroyed, a communist revolution was not possible.

Gramsci and Lukács were both active in the Communist party, but their lives took very different paths. Gramsci was jailed by Mussolini in Italy where he died in 1937 due to poor health. One reason the communazis made Mussolini the fall guy of WWII!

In 1918, Lukács became minister of culture in Bolshevik Hungary. During this time, Lukács realized that if the family unit and sexual morals were eroded, society could be broken down.

Lukács implemented a policy he titled "cultural terrorism," which focused on these two objectives. A major part of the policy was to target children's minds through lectures that encouraged them to deride and reject Christian ethics.

In these lectures, graphic sexual matter was presented to children, and they were taught about loose sexual conduct.

Here again, a Marxist theory had failed to take hold in the real world. The people were outraged at Lukács' program, and he fled Hungary when Romania invaded in 1919.

The Birth of Cultural Marxism

All was quiet on the Marxist front until 1923 when the cultural terrorist turned up for a "Marxist study week" in Frankfurt, Germany. There, Lukács met a young, wealthy Marxist named Felix Weil.

Until Lukács showed up, classical Marxist theory was based solely on the economic changes needed to overthrow class conflict. Weil was enthused by Lukács' cultural angle on Marxism.

Weil's interest led him to fund a new Marxist think tank—the Institute for Social Research. It would later come to be known as simply The Frankfurt School.

In 1930, the school changed course under new director Max Horkheimer. The team began mixing the ideas of Sigmund Freud with those of Marx, and cultural Marxism was born.

In classical Marxism, the workers of the world were oppressed by the ruling classes. The new theory was that everyone in society was psychologically oppressed by the institutions of Western culture. The school concluded that this new focus would need new vanguards to spur the change. The workers were not able to rise up on their own.

As fate would have it, the National Socialists came to power in Germany in 1933. It was a bad time and place to be a Jewish Marxist, as most of the school's faculty was. So, the school moved to New York City, the bastion of Western culture at the time.

<u>Coming to America</u>

In 1934, the school was reborn at Columbia University. Its members began to exert their ideas on American culture.

It was at Columbia University that the school honed the tool it would use to destroy Western culture: the printed word.

The school published a lot of popular material. <u>The first of these was *Critical Theory*.</u>

Critical Theory is a play on semantics. <u>The theory was simple: criticize every pillar of Western culture—family, democracy, common law, freedom of speech, and others. The hope was that these pillars would crumble under the pressure.</u>

"The Drew Carey Show," "The 70s Show," "The Goldbergs," "Mary Hartman, Mary Hartman," "The Cosby Show" "Angel" and the variety of vampire and occult movies, "The Heathers," etc.,etc were full frontal attacks on our mores and manners, our style our substance, our values; and more subtly, even "Little House on the Prairie" played its own role in undermining American values.

And Catholic Universities were silent.

As long as they won the College Football games, hey, everything was ok.

And now Georgetown removes the crucifix in order to appease a rabid pro abort and moslem imposter.

Next was a book Theodor Adorno co-authored, *The Authoritarian Personality.* It redefined traditional American views on gender roles and sexual mores as "prejudice." Adorno compared them to the traditions that led to the rise of fascism in Europe.

Is it just a coincidence that the go-to slur for the politically correct today is "fascist"?

The school pushed its shift away from economics and toward Freud by publishing works on psychological repression.

Their works split society into two main groups: the oppressors and the victims. They argued that history and reality were shaped by those groups who controlled traditional institutions. At the time, that was code for males of European descent.

From there, they argued that the social roles of men and women were due to gender differences defined by the "oppressors." In other words, gender did not exist in reality but was merely a "social construct." The new version is 59 "non-binary" genders! How's that for KHAOS!

A Coalition of Victims

Adorno and Horkheimer returned to Germany when WWII ended. Herbert Marcuse, another member of the school, stayed in America. In 1955, he published *Eros and Civilization*.

In the book, Marcuse argued that Western culture was inherently repressive because it gave up happiness for social progress.

The book called for "polymorphous perversity," a concept crafted by Freud. It posed the idea of sexual pleasure outside the traditional norms. *Eros and Civilization* would become very influential in shaping the sexual revolution of the 1960s.

Marcuse would be the one to answer Horkheimer's question from the 1930s: Who would replace the working class as the new vanguards of the Marxist revolution?

Marcuse believed that it would be a victim coalition of minorities — blacks, women, and homosexuals.

In 21ˢᵗ Century America, the media and too many States and Cities, Universities and Schools, Child "Protective" Services and Family Courts are run by just that VICTIM COALITION OF BLACKS, WOMEN AND HOMOSEXUALS – HOMOSEXUALS AND A VARIETY OF DEVIANTS.

The social movements of the 1960s — black power, feminism, gay rights, sexual liberation — gave Marcuse a unique vehicle to release cultural Marxist ideas into the mainstream. Railing against all things "establishment," The Frankfurt School's ideals caught on like wildfire across American universities.

Marcuse then published *Repressive Tolerance* in 1965 as the various social movements in America were in full swing. In it, he argued that tolerance of all values and ideas meant the repression of "correct" ideas. It was here that Marcuse coined the term "liberating tolerance." It called for tolerance of any ideas coming from the left but intolerance of those from the right. One of the overarching themes of the Frankfurt School was total intolerance for any viewpoint but its own. That is also a basic trait of today's political-correctness believers.

To quote Max Horkheimer, *"Logic is not independent of content."*

<u>Recalling the Words of Winston (Not That One)</u>

The Frankfurt School's work has had a deep impact on American culture. It has recast the homogenous America of the 1950s into today's divided, animosity-filled nation.

In turn, this has contributed to the undeniable breakdown of the family unit, as well as identity politics, radical feminism, and racial polarization in America.

It's hard to decide if today's culture is more like Orwell's 1984 or Huxley's Brave New World.

Never one to buck a populist trend, the political establishment in America has fully embraced the ideas of the Frankfurt School and has pushed them on American society through public miseducation.

Read Full Article Here...

Re Eric Holder:

https://twitter.com/hlaurora63/status/1050360003150929920

He was among the armed rioters that took over the ROTC office. Not surprising that this slug became the only Attorney General to ever be held in contempt of Congress. Surprised that he's ENCOURAGING violence? Not a damn bit!

ABOUT THE AUTHOR
Dr. Deirdre McNamara is a Hahnemannian Homeopath, a dramatist, composer and author.

She took made her first TV appearance on RTE aged 11, took Company Class with the Bolshoi Ballet as a young teenager, represented the RAD at a concert in the Mansion House and won many awards and scholarships in both academia and the arts.

Her dramas were produced on NY's Off-Off Broadway stages, where she won standing ovations for her interpretations of the works of James Joyce and the gentle Welshman, Dylan Thomas.

She is the first Homeopath in a century to consult on critical care, respiratory dependent, antibiotic resistant and hemiplegic conditions.

She treated a community of recovering drug addicts - all her Hep A, B, C patient there are completely free of viral load – and she was the Homeopathic Consultant for St Mother Teresa's Missionaries of Charity in NY.

She has broadcast on radio, BBC, RTE, Shake and Wake, etc., been interviewed by RT, CNN, RTE, Xinhua, etc.

She has composed classic and liturgical music which have been performed in a number of venues, including St Peter's College, New Jersey, and Newburgh Public Library, performed by the great American soprano, Claudia Cummings and has been hugged by Pavarotti, Placido Domingo, Mirella Freni, Giancarlo Menotti and both Leonard and Elmer Bernstein!

Her literary work up to the turn of the Millennium is archived in the National Library of Ireland. Her literary and dramatic output - under stringent conditions - approach forty plays, dramas, novels, mss.

Published works by Deirdre McNamara include: "Child Sexual Abuse – Never Call It Love;" "SOS – For Survivors of Suicides," "The Sanity of Christ vs the Fallacies of Freud," "Meditations on the Mysteries of the Rosary," "The Tuscany Express," " Celebrity City," "The Demise of Senator Duff," "The Disguise" (90 minute Christmas drama written for fundraising purposes,) "The Famine Report," "Tom and the Happy Cat," "Tomas agus an Cat Sasta," Blackie the Bear meets Haggis, etc.

Produced dramas: An Evening with James Joyce and Friends, "Bloomsday!" (First time Joyce was performed at Symphony Space) The Hunger Grass, Mistletoe, Sweet Dreams. Staged reading "The Mercy of Khaled and Nine Eleven."

Original music compositions performed at St Peter's College, St Elizabeth's Church, St Clement's Theatre, etc. Newburgh Library Auditorium – sung by the great American soprano, Claudia Cummings.

Many more works in progress…and in process of restoration. All of the above without grants or subsidies - minimal support – and considerable opposition from the mediocrity which inevitably accompanies corruption.

www.ladybard.wordpress.com
www.drdeirdrehomeopath.weebly.com